D0459163

A GOOD EXAMPLE OF A WELL FITTED DOUBLE BRIDLE

(Miss I. A. Ferrier's Champion Hack, "Warwick" Adelaide Royal Show.)

(This is an excellent example of a well fitted double bridle: evidently made to measure for this particular horse.)

Details

THE BRIDOON AND BIT HEADSTALL BUCKLES, are in the ideal position i.e., about in line with the horse's eye. With the buckles at this height the bridle allows for maximum adjustment, in this case some four or five holes either up or down. Too often the cheek pieces of the headstalls are cut excessively long and the head*stall* correspondingly short.

The Bridoon headstall, which has only one adjusting buckle is assembled with the buckle on the OFF side; which is correct with a double bridle. This is an exception to the general rule — "all adjusting buckles on the near side" but confirms what is stressed throughout these pages — "What is BEST is RIGHT or correct." If assembled on the near side there are four buckles near the one spot and they tend to ride one on top of another. As this can cause discomfort to the horse, one of the four — this one — is removed to the off side. The bridoon is well up into the corners of the lips.

The Bit, including its curbchain is below the bridoon. The lipstrap is loose and its buckle, not visible in the photo, is placed on the near side.

The Curbchain is fitted with a chain guard, which although not essential makes for the comfort of the horse. The unused curb link is neatly hooked up. (For the correct fitting of the curbchain read Chapter 12.)

The throatlash, browband and noseband are all loose fitting and comfortable. The headstall is split at exactly the correct height so that the angle of the throatlash after bifurcation allows the browband to drop clear of the ears but without allowing it to drop so far as to drag the headstall forward against the back of the ears — where it can worry the horse and start him head-tossing. (See Chapter 2.)

The top or bridoon rein is slightly wider than the bottom or Bit rein. The reason for this being so is given in Chapter 15 on "Reins and Running reins."

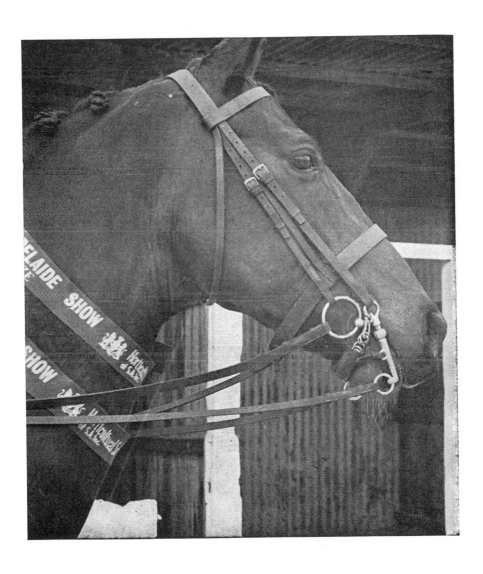

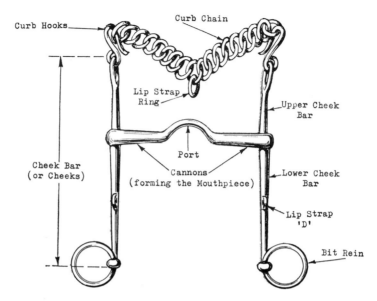

A BIT has a Curb and can act only by Leverage Action.

PARTS OF JOINTED OR BROKEN PELHAM.

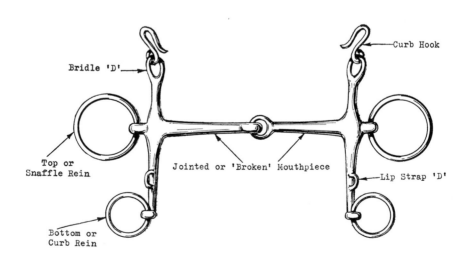

Except for the Mouthpiece and the Upper Rein,
all the other parts are the same as for the Bit.

HORSE CONTROL AND THE BIT

HORSE CONTROL
and
THE BIT

•

TOM ROBERTS

1st Edition 1971
2nd Edition 1973
3rd Edition 1975
4th Edition 1977
5th Edition 1979
6th Edition 1982
7th Edition 1985

and
Should be read before or in conjunction with:
"HORSE CONTROL — THE YOUNG HORSE"
[The Handling, Breaking-in and Early Schooling of Your Own Young Horse]
1st Edition 1974
2nd Edition 1977
3rd Edition 1980
4th Edition 1985

and

"HORSE CONTROL — THE RIDER"
1st Edition 1980
2nd Edition 1982

and

"HORSE CONTROL REMINISCENCES"
1st Edition 1984

Published by T.A. & P.R. Roberts,
241 West Beach Road, Richmond 5033, South Australia.
Aust. Standard Book No. ISBN 0 9599413-0-4

Wholly set up and printed by
Tilbrook Bros. — Northern Argus, Clare, S.A.
Registered at the G.P.O., Adelaide, for
transmission by post as a book.

ACKNOWLEDGEMENTS

I would like to thank those who have helped me in their own different ways. To mention them all is quite out of the question—but they range from the High School rider, Mr. FRANZ MAIRINGER; that fine horseman HAVILDAR MUSTAPHA KHAN of the Indian Cavalry; to Australian horsemen, no less artists in their way such as Mr. DANNY FITZGERALD of Cummins, South Australia.

I have looked and listened and have thought over what I have seen and heard; and have learned that no one method is perfect or even best in all branches of horsemanship. I hope some of what I have learned and written here will assist those who may be puzzled by different styles and different bits. There are reasons for almost every diffrence.

I thank, too, all those who have assisted me with the photos of horse and gear, particularly the late Mr. BRIAN CURTIN, who is responsible for the great majority of the best of the photographs and for which he would accept no payment, and Mrs. NORA BONCEY, who is responsible for all the excellent sketches — she, too, accepted the task as a pleasure.

But most of all I have to thank MY WIFE, PAT. An Australian of one of the oldest families of South Australia, she rode her pony to school — and everywhere else — good tempered always, critical yet helpful and never anything but encouraging, Pat must have typed the MS a dozen times or more! Really, this work is Pat's as much as mine.

CONTENTS

LIST OF ILLUSTRATIONS

INTRODUCTION

If you are interested in the easy control of a horse, the following pages will almost certainly be of help to you. The training, including mouthing or re-mouthing of a horse, is primarily a matter of skill and knowledge but a well-designed and suitable bit will help the task tremendously. A good horseman will do a better job if his tools are first class too.

Bits of many types are reviewed. Some are recommended without reserve; others for special types of horses or for certain classes of work. A good deal will also be said about how to use the bit in the horse's education, and this requires that we understand the main principles of horse training. This, too, will be dealt with.

The work is by no means limited to bits but also includes chapters covering most of the accessories used to control the horse, such as—drop nosebands, martingales, running reins, head checks and reins of all kinds.

In separate chapters special difficulties such as "Tongue over the bit"; "One-sided-mouthed-horses"; "Obtaining a fast halt," etc. are dealt with.

Chapter 11 on "Port Mouths" may, and probably will, provoke a storm of protest at first. But the truth is so manifest, can be so clearly checked and proved, that after the first shock it may be accepted immediately. The full implications are not yet clear. It may well open a new epoch in bit design.

No bit that hurts a horse or makes him uncomfortable when he is behaving in a normal and proper manner will be recommended, for it is the very essence of good horsemanship that the horse should be able to obtain comfort by doing that which we ask of him. It should "pay" him to behave.

Fear and the expectation or anticipation of pain, has possibly an even worse effect than pain itself, and one of the most important tasks with a spoilt mouth is to rid the horse of any fearful anticipation to which he may have become subject.

All mouths are not the same, any more than all heads are the same shape. No one bit will suit every mouth and very few bits suit all riders at all times. What is written here should explain why this is so, and help you to select the most suitable bit for you and your horse.

Almost everything written here has been and is still being proved by the writer's own experience of well over half a century.

CHAPTER 1

THE BASIC PRINCIPLE OF ALL HORSE TRAINING

"Natural" and "unnatural" mouths: First principle of training:
Horses difficult to stop or steady in pace: Excitable or "go-ey" horses

It is astonishing how many riders hold the quite erroneous conviction that it is natural for a horse to stop or decrease his pace if pain is applied to his jaw, yet accept it as being equally natural for the same animal to move forward or increase his pace if pain is applied to almost any other part of his body. Of course this is not natural — the horse has to be taught to respond that way.

Horses with Hard Mouths

Sooner or later such people meet a horse that they consider to be "unnatural"; one which fails to stop, or which actually increases its pace or even runs away, when the pressure on its jaw is increased to an insufferable degree. They cannot understand it; they fail to realise that the *horse does not understand* what is wanted of him.

These riders think their horse's jaw must be insensitive or "hard"; and although they meet with no success they remain firm in the conviction that if only they were stronger, could pull harder, could hurt the horse more, or could get a bit or other device that would hurt him more, success in stopping him would follow.

Nothing could be further from the truth. Every horse has to be taught that one kind of irritation, inconvenience or pain — whip, spur or pressure of the leg etc. — can be avoided by moving forward, and that pressure on another spot, his jaw, can be avoided if he checks his pace. It is so easy for an inexperienced rider unwittingly to lead the horse to believe that all pain means "go" or increase the pace.

A trained horse, a horse with a good mouth, has been taught by someone that when he decreases his pace any pressure or pain from the bit will also decrease. It is not natural for a horse to know this; it has to be taught him, and horses learn from experience. Almost always and only, from experience.

A horse does not stop *because* you worry or hurt his mouth, he stops in order to *avoid* the worry or hurt of the bit. If stopping or slowing does no good he eventually tries something else. If rearing, or bounding, or bolting, etc., is effective in stopping you irritating him, that is the lesson

1

he learns, i.e. that rearing or whatever it is that he does, voids the pain or irritation; it is, therefore, a sensible, natural and, from his point of view, a good thing to do.

First Principle of all Horse Training

When training a horse, we do something (with our hands or legs usually) as an indication to the horse of what we want him to do. What our next action will be depends upon his reaction. If he *tends* by the slightest degree to do what we want, then it is for us to encourage him in that tendency. We usually do this by *immediately decreasing* the irritation or the strength of whatever we were doing.

If on the other hand the horse tends to react in a way that is not desired, we should immediately discourage him in that tendency. In such a case we either quietly maintain the indication and let him realise that relief is not to be obtained by the response he has made, or in some instances we slightly increase the strength of whatever indication we gave in the first place — put a little more pressure on the rein or a little more weight with the legs.

The inconvenience of what we do should fall a good deal short of pain while the horse is under instruction. It is only much later on, when he knows what is wanted and does not obey, that we think of disciplining him by becoming sharp with either hand or leg.

A horse that is difficult to control is almost always so because he does not understand what is wanted of him — *almost* always. But horses who have learned to intimidate their riders by misbehaving, have to be sharply disciplined if they continue with their tricks once they have had proper instruction. Remember, however, that first we have to establish an understanding, and then show him "crime does not pay" if that becomes necessary. A more severe bit is not needed to do this.

Horses Difficult to Stop or Steady in Pace

Quite a big percentage of horses difficult to check down — to get to go on at a slower pace — are comparatively easy to stop. They understand "go," and they understand "stop"; but they do not understand "Steady, but don't stop."

Getting some horses to steady down and continue on with a light hold on the bit when moving in company, as in hunting, etc., is a real problem. Hanging on to him or hurting him more does nothing to improve the situation.

When the pressure on the bit is increased to ask for a stop or decrease of pace, each slight easing of the pace by the horse should be met by the reward or encouragement of a slight but definite lightening of the bit pressure. This lightening of the contact may be only momentary at first, for many horses will immediately start to increase the pace again the moment the reins are lightened. In that case, back we have to go again to the original pressure.

2

In these early stages of re-mouthing, don't think in terms of "give and take" or "pull and loosen"; try only for a LIGHTER rein, not a loose one. Be content with a little progress and encourage that, rather than demand success and reward only that. PROGRESS IS SUCCESS.

Feel for and encourage every tendency the horse shows to relax and decrease pace when you ask for it. If in your efforts to encourage him you reduce the weight on the reins by, say 1/10th and he immediately goes off again, don't be discouraged yourself. Try again, and this time try reducing the rein-weight by only 1/20th. It is for you to find what concession you can make. Persist.

Your horse might be frightened or upset or both. It depends a great deal on his past impressions. You may have to repeat the encouragements time after time, maybe scores of times, until he grasps what you are trying to tell him. Remaking a spoiled mouth is much more difficult and requires much more skill and patience than just putting a good mouth on a young horse.

Excitable or "Go-ey" Horses

One of the greatest and most common mistakes made by riders of lively, excitable, or "go-ey" horses is that they never use their legs. They never "tell" the horse to go.

I can imagine many who read this thinking: "Tell him to go? My trouble is to stop him going. I never have to tell him to go!"

Therein lies the source of many a trouble.

When you want a faster pace at any time, all you need to do and almost certainly all you do, is to loosen or lighten the reins a trifle and off he goes. You just *let* him go.

This means that your horse has come to understand (or has learned by experience, it would be more correct to say, which means you or someone else has taught him) that a loosening of the reins means "go faster." How now can you complain because he does what you have taught him?

If he could talk, I wouldn't be surprised if he said to his rider: "Now, make up your mind what you want. You want me to go faster when you lighten or loosen the reins or you want me *not* to go faster?"

When I get such a horse to re-educate, I start off to let him know that a loosening or lightening of the reins does NOT mean to "go faster." When I want him to go faster I will always, always, ALWAYS tell him, by pressing a little with my legs. I want him to understand quite clearly, "From now on my loosening the reins will only mean you can relax. Just relax."

Such horses as these are willing horses; they are too willing. They are on edge all the time — as if saying "Is it time (to go) yet?" "Is it time yet?" Using your legs whenever you want more pace or energy from your horse in effect says to him: "Relax, settle down. I'll TELL you quite clearly when I do want you to go. I'll give a light pressure with my legs."

Avoid Sudden Pulls on the Reins. Be sure you avoid suddenly tightening the reins when he "shoots off" after you have tried for a lighter rein contact. If you re-tighten the reins with a jerk he will quickly come to see your lightening of the rein pressure, not as a reward but as a preliminary to a jerk on his mouth. Remember, he learns from his experience and not by thinking as we do.

Don't Pull. Note that throughout these pages I carefully avoid the use of the word. "pull." A pull is a "continuing drawing toward you of your hand." It makes a horse into a puller, for the horse gains nothing by yielding to a pulling hand; such a hand continues to "take" after the horse has given.

Punish and reward? No: *Encourage and discourage*! So many people will say "You must give and take," but fail to say when to give and when to take. Others say "Punishment and reward is the secret" and although this is rather more helpful it is not quite right either.

Punishment and reward are too far apart — they are the extremes of encouragement and discouragement. Between these two extremes are scores of graduated leg or rein pressures that decrease as the horse tends to do what we require of him; or increase, or more often than not are repeated or persisted with, if he should fail to respond as desired.

Between right and wrong, the horse may show innumerable *tendencies towards* right and wrong. These tendencies are readily detectable if you learn to feel for them. The better horseman is the one who is always alert to feel what is happening under him. There is a saying: "He sends you a telegram." But only if you are alert to "feel," will you get the message. This is the great difference between the "natural" horseman and those less fortunate. The "born horseman" senses or feels what the horse is *going to do* and so is far ahead of those who wait to see WHAT HE HAS DONE. The better horseman prevents mistakes; the other corrects them.

Get your horse calm; keep your horse calm. To improve, a horse must learn; and to learn he must be calm. A sharp bit and the consequent pain from it destroys calmness.

Fear of pain continues long after the cause ceases, and it takes quite a while for the average horse to get over this fear once he has been mishandled. Until his fears are allayed he will not be calm, and he will not improve. So even when you are doing all you should, it will still take a while before such a horse responds. He will still fear a recurrence of previous pain.

A change of bit is often to be recommended. Occasionally a change of bit is all that is required. BUT . . . to which bit?

This is the problem I can help you with.

4

CHAPTER 2

CAUSES AND RESULTS OF DISTRACTION

Distraction can help—or hinder—training: Bridle can distract:
Saddle can distract: Racehorses that will not face Barrier:
Correct Saddle Fitting

Things that distract a horse's attention can be both a blessing and a curse. Everyone, I suppose, knows the value of a "twitch" and the principle on which it works. How, by drawing the horse's attention to his top lip by the twitch, we can often dress an injury etc. which he would not let us get near without its use. He does not notice what we are doing because we have distracted his attention elsewhere. Distraction, or counter-attraction, can be used to advantage in many ways.

When we are training a horse or teaching him anything at all, it will pay us to check and be sure that a distraction is not working against us.

I do not intend to give a lecture here on the fitting of saddle or bridle, but I feel I should warn you that a thorough understanding of the principles governing good gear fitting is an absolute essential if you wish to enjoy good sport on the back of a horse.

Nothing we put on the horse should cause him pain or discomfort as long as he is behaving in a proper manner — doing what we want of him. That does not mean to say that we will never hurt him; we will find it necessary to discipline him occasionally; but even this will be more effective if there is not already some other constant or nagging pain or discomfort bothering and distracting him.

Most of us have good cause to remember the discomfort a tight shoe can cause, although when first put on the shoe might have felt quite comfortable. We know how irritating it can become after a time and how it can distract our attention from other matters we have thought important.

So it is with our horse. We cannot expect him to attend to light changes of pressure of bit and leg if there is something else worrying him more. It is for us to see that he is not distracted in this way.

Where bones are not well padded with flesh, such as our feet and the horse's head, withers and spine, it takes very little pressure to cause great discomfort if the pressure is maintained for long.

5

The Bridle

The bridle has only one real purpose: to keep the bit in the horse's mouth at the height we require it. A single strap, the bit headstall, would do that. To the headstall we usually add a browband in the front to stop it slipping back on to the horse's neck, and a throatlash at the rear to check it slipping forward over his ears. Both the throatlash and the browband can cause trouble if too tight—too short (see Figure 2 page 10).

Perhaps you might think these are trifles that have nothing whatever to do with your horse giving you trouble one way or another. Then let me draw your attention to any picture you may have of a horse from the Spanish Riding School in Vienna. Notice how loose the browband is, noticeably loose. Notice, too, that they do not use a throatlash. Even the younger horses ridden on a snaffle and drop-noseband use a bridle fitted only with a jowl strap. *They* consider these things important.

A short browband will draw the bit-headstall forward against the back of the horse's ears, which means that its edges will be pressing against the base of the ears for perhaps hours. Watch how your horse appreciates you rubbing that particular spot when you dismount — even when the browband is comfortably long!

The throatlash should be as thin as it is possible to get it, as it can become pinched between the jaw and the neck when the horse arches his neck well. Either leave it off, like the Spanish School, or have it very thin and loose.

The Saddle

This is a book mainly dealing with bits and the horse's mouth — and it may surprise you that I should stress that it is important that you fully understand the rules of saddle fitting. It is a fact, however, that your horse will not even notice what you are doing with the bit if the saddle or other gear is worrying him more. To get good responses — the best — from him, we should see that everything fits him comfortably. The saddle should not distract his attention like the twitch.

A good and well-fitting saddle keeps all weight off the withers and other bony projections of the spine so that no part of the saddle even *touches* these sparsely covered bones. It should spread the rider's weight over the muscles on each side of the spine and spread it evenly.

The saddle is built on a saddle-tree which consists of sidebars of wood shaped and sloped to conform to the shape of the back of the particular horse. The sidebars for a wide horse with well-sprung ribs will, of course, need to be set at a different angle than will one for a narrow-chested animal.

The sidebars are kept in place each side of the spine by a front and rear arch of steel. The front arch must be high enough to clear the withers by a good margin, and the rear arch not so high, as it only has to clear the

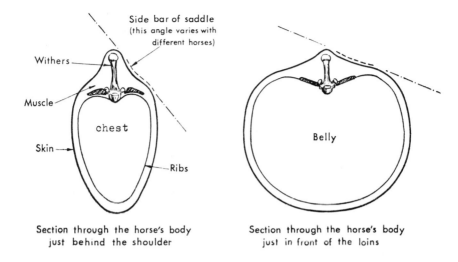

Side bar of saddle
(this angle varies with
different horses)

Withers

Muscle

chest

Skin

Ribs

Belly

Section through the horse's body
just behind the shoulder

Section through the horse's body
just in front of the loins

Figure 1.

spine. The tree, padded on the underneath of the sidebars for the comfort of the horse, and covered with leather and shaped on the upper surface for the comfort of the rider, more or less makes the saddle.

The great thing for us to remember is that the sidebars must be set at a suitable angle for the horse on which it is to be used, and then padded, and that there are *two steel arches that must be kept clear of the spine.* If these arches are not *well clear* of the bones, you will certainly have trouble coming up.

Notice that I say: "well clear." If, when you are sitting in the saddle, you cannot run your finger or at least a pencil under the front arch from one side and then over the top of the wither and down the other, you are taking risks, *for the clearance does not remain constant.* That is the very minimum clearance, and the pencil should be able to reach at least two inches under the arch.

Remember that the saddle which carries you rests on the muscles, and that these muscles contract and relax as the horse moves and the saddle raises and lowers accordingly. Each time the muscles relax they become a little thinner and the saddle drops a fraction. Every time the horse puts his feet to the ground the rider's weight presses down a little more under the impact — and again the steel arch gets closer to the bone. This is particularly so when the horse is jumping and, to a lesser degree, when galloping.

If the steel front arch is not WELL CLEAR it often nips the horse's spine as his weight drops on to his front legs after a jump or a galloping stride. Of course the higher the fence and the steeper the angle at which the horse meets the ground, the more the saddle will compress the muscles

7

under the rider's weight and, if the steel front arch is too close, the more it will bite into the horse's wither.

It would be interesting to know how many horses that start refusing over big "straight" fences, do so from fear of the pain of an ill-fitting saddle.

Another factor is that when a horse is pulling firmly on the bit, there is actually more weight in the saddle. Not a great deal, it is true, but all these things add together and when they all operate in unison the saddle causes the horse sudden stabs of pain — unless the arch is WELL CLEAR of the withers. It may only occur occasionally, but fear of pain is almost as bad as the pain itself.

Racehorses that Won't Face the Barrier

How many racehorses are discarded from racing because they cannot be brought to face the barrier? I find almost invariably that the animal is either high-withered or narrow-backed—the latter permits the saddle to drop lower.

A racing saddle is made as light as possible — but it should not be at the expense of the clearance of the animal's withers. Whatever is reduced, it should not be this, for the saddle can easily drop a quarter of an inch when the horse is galloping and even more if he is jumping.

If packing is used under the saddle, it should be placed under the side-bars *not* under the pommel. The saddle and the arch have to be raised, not the arch filled in, which would put even more weight on the withers.

These horses that won't face the barrier can become really difficult to control, and, as with all difficult horses, our attention should first be directed to a search for painful points that may be tormenting him. The racehorse may be more worried over what the saddle will do to his back when he begins galloping, than what the jockey does. No fine-spirited animal would want to race under these conditions.

All this is to stress that the trouble you may feel at your horse's mouth may have its origin in a completely different location.

Saddle Fitting

Here are the main guide-rules for saddle fitting as there are sure to be some readers who are not clear about them:

1. The withers must not be pinched or pressed upon.
Note: "pressed" means downward pressure as from the weight in the saddle, but "pinched" means sideways pressure on the sides of the withers due to the front arch not being wide enough. In these cases the edges of the sidebars rest on the sides of the base of the withers. This space at the *sides* should not be filled in with excessive packing.
2. There must be no pressure on the spine.
3. There must be no weight on the loins.

4. The saddle should rest sufficiently far back as not to interfere with the free play of the shoulder-blades.

Note: the top of the shoulderblade comes back as the point of the shoulder moves forward.

5. The whole of the weight should be *evenly distributed* over the ribs through the medium of the muscles covering them.

The saddle should always be fitted without any packing under it when looking to see how it fits. You cannot see how it fits when you have a felt or a sheepskin under it.

A ¼″ is the absolute minimum of clearance with a rider up, for remember the saddle will drop if the horse loses weight at any time. Packing in the panel under the saddle also settles and drops after a few months' regular wear and a new saddle should then be taken back to the saddler for correction by the addition of more packing. This is necessary with all saddles— even the most expensive.

I often wonder whether we will ever see a onepiece moulded saddletree of something like fibre glass. It might even incorporate the seat and do away with the front and rear arches.

CHAPTER 3

SNAFFLES — BITS — PELHAMS — DOUBLE BRIDLES
What are the differences? Which bit is best?

THE MAIN GROUPINGS OF BITS

What is a — Snaffle? — Bit? — Pelham? — Double Bridle?

The term "bit" is applied generally to anything that is placed in a horse's mouth with the object of controlling him. In this respect it is confusing at times as it also has a more limited meaning; just as the term "horse" can apply to a mare, gelding, filly, colt or horse, so the term "bit" may refer to a Snaffle, Bit or Pelham. Every one of the hundreds and hundreds of bits to be found, falls into one or other of these groups.

SNAFFLES AND BRIDOONS

Figure 2.

*Showing a snaffle.
The rein pressure goes straight to the horse's mouth without leverage.
Note the step taken to avoid discomforting the horse with a tight browband. The horse's comfort always comes before appearances.
Note too, the method of attaching the headstall to the noseband. This and any similar method that causes a projection to the inside of the noseband should be avoided. Read more about this in Chapter 14 on Standing Martingales.*

Snaffles, including the small snaffle known as the bridoon, are of innumerable shapes, sizes, types, designs and materials. They all have this in common — any force applied to the snaffle by means of the hands and reins acts *directly* on the horse's mouth. What is meant by "directly" might be better understood if I said that a snaffle has no leverage or pulley action like curb and gag bits (for Gag Bits see Figures 33 to 36 pages 38 and 39).

Only one rein is necessary with a snaffle, although two are often used and will be recommended in certain circumstances — for instance when a running martingale or a gag bit is used.

BITS

Throughout these pages when "Bit" is spelt with a capital "B",
we mean it to have its more limited meaning as in the following paragraph.
There is probably an even greater variety of Bits than of snaffles. All Bits
have this in common: any pressure from the reins reaches the mouth

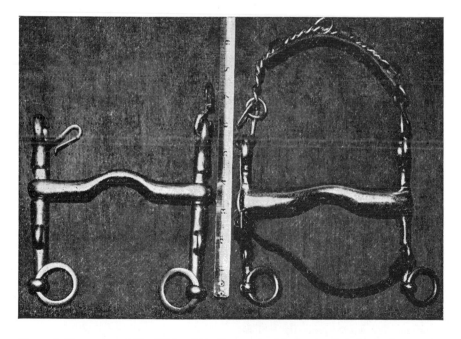

Figure 3. Two types of Bit. With a Bit, all contact with the mouth is by the lever action of the cheek-bar. The rule between shows lengths and proportions.
Notice the carefully made curb hooks on the Bit with the fixed cheek, which is discussed in Chapter 10.

11

indirectly. To be a "Bit" in its more restricted use, it must be so designed and the rein or reins attached in such a position, that any tension on the reins reaches the mouth only by lever action. The rein or the reins of a Bit must be attached to a bar or cheek which acts as a lever, the mouthpiece being the fulcrum acting on the bars of the mouth (to be quite correct, the curb chain is the fulcrum from which the leverage is applied to the mouth-piece).

It is usual to use only one rein on a Bit, but two are occasionally used on some types.

PELHAMS

A pelham in its many variations is a type of bit combining the action of both snaffle and Bit. The pelham is of necessity designed to be used with two reins, one of which (the top rein) will have a snaffle or direct action; the other, the bottom rein, will have the indirect action of leverage on the mouth, which is the characteristic of a Bit (see Figure 4).

Figure 4.
A Pelham with Vulcanite
Mouthpiece.
The top rein acts directly on
the mouth—without leverage.
The bottom-indirectly—or by
a leverage. Peter Whynte's
"Kirton Point."

Summarising

To be a snaffle the tension on the reins must be transmitted to the horse's mouth direct. An ounce of weight at the finger tips will equal an ounce weight at the horse's mouth. Both reins, if there are more than one, must act directly on the mouth.

To be a Bit any tension on the reins must reach the mouth indirectly, and a curb of some sort is essential. Both reins, if there are more than one, must work by indirect action alone, i.e. by a lever action through the

12

medium of the curb and the mouthpiece. An ounce weight at the fingertips may be converted by the lever into several times that weight at the horse's mouth — or *it may not be increased at all,* depending upon the proportions of the lever arm. This last point is important, but it is often overlooked.

THE DOUBLE BRIDLE

The double bridle is one that is fitted with two bits. It has a snaffle and a curb bit on the one bridle, with a separate rein to each. When a snaffle is used in conjunction with a Bit in this manner, it changes its name and is called a "bridoon." So a double bridle consists of a bridle with two bits fitted, a "Bit and Bridoon," both in the mouth at the same time.

Figure 5.
Miss Ann Holdcroft's "Golden Summit" showing a double bridle. The bridoon has direct action only, and the Bit leverage action only.

Pelham Never Takes Place of Double Bridle

In theory, the pelham combines the effects of the two bits of a double bridle. But in actual practice it does not do so.

On a pelham, the top rein *used alone* does produce the effect of a snaffle, and the bottom rein *used alone* does produce the effect of a Bit — but the two reins *used together* somehow do not produce the effects of a double bridle.

Without doubt the two separate bits of a double bridle somehow speak more plainly than the combination, and so the pelham will not be recommended here to take the place of a double bridle. The pelham is, however, to be recommended for use in the place of a snaffle *or as a snaffle* when the ordinary snaffle has been tried and has been proved to be unsatisfactory For this, as for everything else recommended or condemned, reasons are given (see Chapters 7 and 8).

13

WHICH BIT IS THE BEST?

The best is the one that WORKS best. It will vary with each combination of horse, rider and occasion. This is applicable to most other disputed points about riding: the "right" length of stirrup to use, the "right" way to hold the reins, the "right" way to mount, the "right" way to sit in the saddle — what is BEST for that particular occasion is right, and it changes from one occasion to another.

A man trying to establish a high jump record will cheerfully risk a fall to succeed; the same man jumping or, say, hunting for pleasure, will not unnecessarily take the same risk. One he may consider justified and the other not, and he will sit and ride differently.

The demands made on a horse during a race are very different from those made during a game of polo etc., and we will show it to be advisable to sometimes change the bit from one occasion to the other.

This is certain however: whatever the bit we use, it should not be painful to the horse at the time we make an exacting demand upon him. The pain will distract his attention and cause him to stiffen or lock muscles, thus preventing him from acting in the most efficient manner. This does not necessarily mean that a bit should never hurt the horse. On a disobedient horse we sometimes need a bit capable of becoming sharp — but it should not become sharp in ordinary use.

If your horse goes well on the bit you are using for the job you are doing, stick to it. If you are having trouble and hope that a change of bit will help, first read these pages and then try a mild bit of the type recommended. I need hardly say that before you start, you should be sure the horse is sufficiently educated for the job you have in mind.

The Snaffle . . .

A snaffle is recommended for straightforward work where no sharp and sudden demands are made with the reins. It is recommended for racing, and for the young horse. For these tasks the snaffle is best because of its mild simplicity.

The Pelham . . .

A pelham of a recommended type is often found best for the horse that may have sharp and sudden demands upon his mouth as in an exciting game or pursuit. A pelham and certain of the Bits that can mildly lock on the jaw are often found to be best in these circumstances, where the hands of a rider are frequently and unintentionally rough. (See Chapter 7).

Pelhams and curb bits of any kind are not suited for horses that "lean on the bit"; for such horses like to get the bit locked and still on their jaw in the one position, so that they can lean on it with comfort. This type of horse is better with a snaffle, and a hand that will keep the bit mobile on his jaw — a snaffle or possibly a double bridle.

14

The Double Bridle . . .

A double bridle is usually found best for the finished and finely trained horse and when used by a rider who is able to give the aids his undivided attention, such as in dressage or any exhibition or show riding. Probably nothing else is quite so good or quite so accurate. It is the best for the task.

It is well to know, however, that most of the *training* of a finely trained horse intended to be shown in a double bridle, is done on a snaffle. Even when the horse is "on the double bridle" most of the exercising and schooling is done on a snaffle. The earlier lessons are still practised — they are the foundations, and must be maintained.

CHAPTER 4

THE HEAD — AND ABNORMALITIES THAT CAUSE TROUBLE WITH BITS

Top jaw is wider than bottom jaw: Sharp teeth:
Young horses have special tooth troubles: The molars:
Bit faults to avoid: Abnormal mouths: Horses "bad about the head":
Injuries to the jaw

Have you ever considered how awkwardly the horse's head is designed for taking a bit?

In the first place, like most animals his whole head tapers from the ears towards the mouth. It gets narrow from side to side as well as from front to rear. This means that the higher we place the bit, the wider it (the bit) needs to be because the animal's head is wider. It also means that when a curb chain is fitted, the higher in the mouth the bit is placed the greater distance the curb chain has to cover, and the longer it needs to be.

It is not generally recognised that the horse's upper jaw is wider from side to side than the bottom jaw. At the height of the molar teeth the top jaw is much wider, and the outside edges of the top molars are at least $\frac{1}{2}''$ outside the line of the edges of the bottom molars. This difference in the width of the top and bottom jaws at the level of the molars can be readily felt by anyone caring to run their finger over the outside of the skin at that point.

The top molar teeth are themselves also wider from side to side, so that they have a much larger table than the lower. There is good reason for the teeth to be made like this, for the movement of the lower jaw as the horse masticates and grinds up his food, rotates the lower teeth over the surface of the top molars — which therefore need the larger table surface.

To assist the horse to crush his hard tough food, these tables of the back teeth are provided with numerous hard enamel ridges that make both the tables of the teeth *and the edges of the teeth* hard and very sharp. This is an essential and normal condition.

Although this formation assists in mastication, it also poses problems when we come to put a bit in the horse's mouth. Problems that too often are not recognised by the rider.

16

Figure 6.
The horse's top and bottom jaw viewed from below the bottom jaw. (The outer side of the bottom jaw has been painted black to assist in identification.)
The photo clearly shows the extent to which the upper molars project beyond—to the outer side of—the lower teeth. The outer edges of the top molars and the inner edges of the bottom molars are always sharp and rough to some extent.*
These projecting edges of the upper teeth are a hazard that the good horseman never loses sight of. Notice, too, that the first molar runs to a point or edge to the front as does its counterpart.

SHARP TEETH

I suppose every horse-owner has heard of horses developing "sharp teeth" that call for veterinary attention. When this condition occurs, the normally sharp but SHORT sharp edges of the enamel ridges become LONG and sharp. This is due to the bottom jaw not having sufficient movement to enable the bottom teeth to wear down the whole surface of the top molars. The inside edges of the bottom teeth and (this also greatly concerns us with the bit) THE OUTSIDE EDGES OF THE TOP MOLARS BECOME LONG. This

Figure 7.
Part of top jaw taken from the under side showing how sharp are the edges of the top teeth at the outer side. This jaw is normal: In cases of "sharp teeth" the outer points become very much longer. It may be over such sharp points the martingale draws the sides of the noseband.

17

frequently interferes with the horse's mastication and it becomes necessary to have the teeth rasped level if he is to maintain condition. We will find it also causes trouble with some bits.

Summarising

Before we go on with the special troubles a young horse may have with his teeth, we must remember that the top molars of all horses are wider than the bottom by more than ½″ each side; that the edges are always sharp to some degree; and that under certain conditions the sharp points can also become very long. This applies to all horses, and more particularly to those *over* 7 years of age.

YOUNG HORSES HAVE SPECIAL TOOTH TROUBLES

The Molars

Most horsemen know of the changes that occur in the front teeth of a young horse, the incisors, and that up to some six or seven years of age they provide a fairly accurate guide to the animal's age.

But, many riders overlook or do not know of the even greater changes that take place among the back teeth of all horses up to 4½ years, and that the teeth and the gums at the back are frequently very sore and tender due to this teething.

During this period not only are 12 temporary or "milk" molars being replaced by the much larger permanent teeth, but 12 *more* of these great permanent molars — making 24 in all — are forming and forcing their way through the still growing jawbone.

These permanent molars are REALLY BIG and not only in section, for they usually exceed 4½″ in length. Twenty-four of these enormous teeth are bedded into the comparatively small jaws and by the time the horse is about 4½ years of age, have forced their way into his mouth. In many cases — quite often in fact — the jaw is not big enough to hold them and frequently the teeth can be seen bulging through the underside of the lower jaw of 3-4 year olds, causing unsightly enlargements. You have probably noticed these lumps under the jaw, some 2″-3″ above the chin groove, for they often detract from the appearance of the young horse's head.

So, in addition to the threat to his comfort of the sharp edges of the molars throughout the life of every horse, at the same widest part of the head and up to at least 4½ years of age, there is what is often a very painful process going on — teething.

Anyone handling young horses should be well aware of these things; they should never lose sight of the fact that teething can make the mouth and head very tender and sore, and that anything pressing on or even near a sore gum can be exquisitely painful. And again I stress — "At the widest part of the head, at this level."

18

Any part of the bit that extends more than an inch or so above the mouthpiece can be a source of trouble, as almost all bits — certainly all snaffles — tend to work up the jaws towards the molars and the wider part of the head when the reins are stretched.

We can see too, that any pressure on the side of the mouth, high up, will press the lining of the cheek in against these sharp tooth-edges, and if the pressure is strong enough the inside of the cheek will be bruised and torn.

Only too often *the rider knows nothing of what is happening* near the back teeth and wonders why the horse does not attend more to the much less painful and less irritating pressure of the bit on the bars of his mouth.

We should know what to do to avoid pressure on the cheek near the molars — and should know, too, that certain bits and certain other gear have had bad records in this respect. All the following can give trouble:

Bits that work up the mouth at times.
Bits which are the same width at the top of the cheekbar as they are at the mouthpiece.
Bits with a too-long *upper* cheek-bar.
Bits that are designed not to be reversed but which can be put on the wrong way around.
Tight nosebands (other than drop nosebands).
Nosebands that a standing martingale can pull tight.
Nosebands with some part of the headstall projecting to the inside.
Riders who, on occasion, pull hard on one rein.
Stud-fasteners, which project to the inside some ¼" more than the leather they are fastened to.

Each of these will be dealt with later. Bit-makers and designers are well aware of the difficulties and have in most cases provided something to deal with the problem. Our necessity is to get the facts, know the problem and understand which bit will be suitable.

I have said that young horses have special — and additional — troubles when they are teething, but some animals have troubles peculiar only to themselves.

ABNORMAL MOUTHS

The construction of heads varies enormously; teeth, too, are far from being uniform. Some have slight differences but others would warrant the description — "deformed." Some deformities can be seen and recognised easily as they involve the front teeth; a "parrot mouth" for instance, where

19

the front teeth do not meet normally. But often there are deformities further back in the mouth not easily noticed. Such horses almost always profit from regular veterinary inspection.

During World War I, I had to recommend a young mule for destruction for vice. I examined his mouth after he was "put down" (you couldn't get near him while he lived) — poor wretched animal. He had eight teeth on the left side of the lower jaw: two additional teeth were growing one above the other and both jammed between the normal teeth. The lower tooth had pushed the upper one sideways and both had evidently continued to grow. The roots and lower parts of the teeth had burst through the jaw in all directions. The mule must have been almost mad with toothache. An extreme case, it is true, but one that shows the need for inspection of the mouth whenever a horse behaves badly.

HORSES "BAD ABOUT THE HEAD"

Horses that are "bad about the head" should always have special consideration. They may have a very good reason for being so. Perhaps you are unable to inspect the back teeth, but your Vet. can. You should also learn to know and recognise a normal mouth and jaw so that you will recognise any abnormality. Veterinary attention and/or a special bit may be needed.

Remember that almost every snaffle pulls up the mouth towards the molars if the horse pokes his nose out. Whenever this occurs, if there is any flesh or skin of any kind that can be pinched between the bit and the first molar, the horse is going to have a bad time — and he will behave quite out of character when it happens!

Sometimes the gum itself becomes inflamed for one reason or another, and swells in front of the first molar. Occasionally, too, a horse has a lot of loose skin on the bars of his mouth and this moves up when the bit pulls against it, wrinkling up against the front of the first molar. This loose skin can then be pinched by the bit.

Quite often the lip itself is pulled inward by the bit and gets pinched against the tooth; sometimes we meet a horse with *very* thick lips at the sides, which fold inward in the shape of an inverted "L". This can be the source of a great deal of trouble, and a horse with such a mouth seldom goes well in a snaffle. A Bit or pelham with a half-moon or port-mouthed mouthpiece and fitted a little "too wide" for a normal mouth, often suits.

I could quote instance after instance of "bad horses" brought to me for correction of some mouth difficulty, the cause of which I have found to be soreness and in some cases abscesses and ulceration of the membrane and lining of the mouth. This is sometimes the result of an abnormal conformation of the teeth and it is wonderful what a change to a suitable bit can do.

INJURIES TO THE JAW

Whenever a horse pulls back and breaks the bit headstall so that the bit is torn from his mouth, the damage done to his mouth is often much more serious than the damage to the bridle — but is often unobserved. Very, very often the bars of the horse's mouth are cut as the bridle breaks and the bit is torn through: so if he has to be used soon afterwards be sure that the bit is adjusted to avoid the sore spot. Such things as this often lead to troubles that continue long after the injury is healed and forgotten.

A few years ago a valuable show-horse was badly injured and disfigured in a float accident. When his leg injuries were sufficiently healed to permit his being ridden, he was found to be almost uncontrollable. He changed hands after that several times before I was asked to look at him. I found that, probably in the accident, a piece of bone had been broken off the top edge of the bottom jaw bone — the bars — and was hanging by a strip of flesh about ½" wide, loose in the mouth just below the bit. It hardly seems possible that several good horsemen had tackled this horse and not one of them had thought to look to see if all was well and normal with the animal's mouth.

Have you ever thought to look to see, or to feel, what the mouth is like where the bit presses? This part of the jaw, where the bit rests, is called the "bars of the mouth": the "bar" is really the top edge of the jawbone and it, too, varies considerably from horse to horse. Sometimes the ridge is quite rounded — not unlike the bridge of our own nose — but most are very much sharper and many consist of a ridge of bone as sharp as the back edge of a knife. Even a thick bit can cause the horse great pain although it might be used quite lightly (see Figures 54 and 55 page 79).

21

CHAPTER 5

SNAFFLES — TYPES, USES AND FEATURES

Smooth Jointed Ring Snaffle: Egg-Butt Snaffle:"D" Snaffle:
F.M. Snaffle: Spoon Snaffle: Tom Thumb Snaffle:
Ring-in-the-Mouth Snaffle: Key Snaffle or "Mouthing" bit:
Spanish Snaffle: Double Snaffle: "W" Snaffle: Four-ringed Snaffle:
Nose pressure: Soft Rubber Snaffle: Vulcanised Snaffle:
Half-moon and Straight Snaffles: Half-moon Snaffle with Chin Strap:
Gag Snaffles.

The names given to snaffles in these pages are the common ones in every-day use and with few exceptions, such as the Tom Thumb and Spanish Snaffles, are descriptions rather than names — this being the common practice.

The Smooth Jointed Ring Snaffle, for instance, has a smooth mouth-piece with a joint in the centre and fairly large rings for cheeks. The Ring-in-the-Mouth Bar Snaffle is similar to the above, but the two halves of the mouthpiece are joined at the centre by a small ring (see Figure 16 page 28). The "bar" refers to a bar included in the cheeks. An Egg-Butt Snaffle (see Figure 9 page 23) is one in which the joint where cheek and mouthpiece meet is shaped as the name suggests, and so on.

Various bit-makers and designers, however, have given their own names to certain designs, and it is impossible to keep up with all these. Only when a bit is in common use and it is usual to refer to it by a particular name, will that be done.

It is not the purpose of this work to promote or advertise any bit-maker, saddler or type of bit. The aim is to point out the effect of different shapes, thicknesses, actions, etc., so that a student, should he come across some novel feature in a bit, will be able to assess its qualities and/or defects and so form his own conclusions as to its usefulness either for general service or for a specific horse or mouth fault. In this chapter we will deal with snaffles; in the latter part of the book, with curb bits and pelhams.

This is probably the most common of all the snaffles. It is a good useful bit, reasonably cheap to buy — but its mouthpiece is often made too thin. If you are buying one, look for a mouthpiece at least ⅝″ diameter, with large rings which make it more difficult to pull through the mouth should horse and rider come into conflict. This pulling through the mouth of rings and bit can be countered by either a drop nose-band or by passing a light strap (twine or a leather lace will do in an emergency) from ring to ring behind the jaw and above the reins (see Figures 30, 31 and 32 pages 36 and 37). This strap, if used, should be a loose fit and at least as long or even a little longer than the mouthpiece itself.

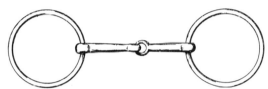

Figure 8.
A Smooth Jointed Ring Snaffle. The one illustrated has seen a lot of service and so is very much worn at the centre joint. The joint should be a close one as in Figure 9 which follows.

Although otherwise quite satisfactory for general use, the ordinary ring snaffle is not recommended for use during the *early* breaking period of a young horse, as there is no way to prevent the centre of the mouthpiece dropping in the mouth (see Tongue over the Bit, Chapter 17).

EGG-BUTT SNAFFLE

There are many varieties of the Egg-Butt Snaffle, almost all being ring snaffles of one kind or another.

In each case, the mouthpiece, instead of being just pierced or drilled to enable the cheek ring to pass through the end, terminates at its outer ends in an egg-shaped enlargement. This is the "egg-butt." It is drilled through and the cheeks fastened to it by means of a steel pin or core passing through its centre. The much-enlarged bearing created by the egg-butt ensures that it does not wear out as quickly as an ordinary ring snaffle.

The ordinary ring snaffle wears at this joint and often pinches the corner of the horse's mouth, causing even a quiet easy-going animal to behave badly. This is much less likely to happen with an Egg-Butt. The longer bearing also keeps the edges of the joint further away from the corner of the horse's lips, thus reducing the chances of pinching.

This is probably the best type of *ring* snaffle — when properly made and where the mouthpiece is fairly thick as it almost invariably is with a quality bit.

Figure 9.
Egg-Butt Snaffle. The larger bearings have a longer life and note, too, the large and well fitting bearing of the centre joint.

Badly Finished Edges

On one occasion, I was using an Egg-Butt Snaffle especially bought for a difficult and very excitable pony, and on re-examining her mouth at the end of the third day's use of the bit, I was surprised to see a small pink spot about one to two inches above the corners of the mouth. I put a rider on the mare and had the reins kept tight while I examined the bridle. A close examination of the snaffle showed that the egg-butt had not been accurately drilled and that this had resulted in a sharp edge being left on the inside at one end. This, by the end of the third day's ride, had chafed the mare's mouth well above where the bit rested when the rein was loose. I took the bit back to the saddler and found, on examination, that of six bits of similar design that he had in stock, only two were free of the same fault.

Absolute accuracy in drilling is evidently difficult and adds to the cost — but there should be no difficulty in machining all surfaces perfectly smooth before leaving the factory. Check, when buying this type of bit, to see that you are not landed with one of the faulty ones. None of the Egg-Butt Snaffles I examined were stamped with the maker's name, which is probably significant.

THE "D" SNAFFLE (see Figure 10 page 25)

This, like the Egg-Butt, is another slight variation of the ring snaffle, the ring being shaped like the letter "D" from which it gets its name. Like the Egg-Butt Snaffle, it aims at neutralising any possible pinching of the lips at the cheek joint by reducing wear and by keeping the edges of the joint away from the corners of the lips.

Unlike the Egg-Butt, however, which, having a big bearing lasts well, the "D" Snaffle usually has a very small bearing at each end of the straight section of the "D".

Although I have never known one of these bits to pinch the lips, they often cause trouble by chafing the skin. You will find that after some use the movable surfaces at the ends of the straight section wear, and can develop very sharp burred or feathered edges which chafe the cheeks of the horse. This causes trouble if the horse is in any way inclined to pull. All snaffles work up the mouth when the reins are tight and this sharp edge, although often so small as to be unnoticed (you will feel it more easily than see it), chafes the outside of the jaw as high as six inches above the corners of the lips — as high, or even higher, than the noseband.

Although these bits serve quite well on horses with nice mouths not given to pulling; as they have nothing the Egg-Butt has not, I see no good reason to recommend them. On the other hand when used on a horse that "takes hold" they can cause real trouble. Of the two, a good Egg-Butt Snaffle is in every way to be preferred.

Figure 10. The "D" Snaffle with protective leather washer. Wear is visible in this snaffle at the point where the "D" and the cheek bar meet. It is not the wear—the gap —that causes trouble with this design; it is the burred-over sharp edge that develops at the spot.
The leather washer is recommended for any bit that can cause pinching or chafing. With the "D" snaffle as shown, it is recommended that the washer be laced to the lower cheek bar to ensure it following the cheek ring when the rein is drawn tight.

"F.M." SNAFFLE

This is a smooth jointed bar snaffle of moderate thickness, enjoying considerable popularity in certain circles throughout Australia today. It has all the good features of the smooth jointed ring snaffle. Like all "Bar" snaffles, it can be prevented from dropping in the centre and does not readily pull through the mouth.

It gets its name in Australia from Mr. Franz Mairinger, the trainer of the Australian Olympic Equestrian Team, who uses no other snaffle. It has been in use in the Spanish Riding School in Vienna for centuries and was also the only snaffle, other than the Key Mouthing Snaffle, issued in the British Army for general use with young horses.

An almost identical bit (Figures 13 and 14 page 27) is to be found on almost all Australian cattle stations, where they have been used for many, many years.

I need hardly say that it is a good snaffle. Its features are:

. . . its mouthpiece is fairly thick and does not taper or curve excessively;

. . . the rings forming the joint of the mouthpiece, the first spot at which a snaffle wears, are also comparatively thick and each fits snugly (not loosely) inside the other;

. . . from the HORSE'S point of view the bit is usually comfortable;

. . . from the RIDER'S point of view it wears well and gives satisfaction.

The top of the cheek bar (full bar as against half-bar) is splayed slightly outwards. This is to allow for the shape of the horse's head, which widens as it goes up and becomes pinched by the top bar if the bar does not conform. A good bar bit of any type always allows for this and the cheek

25

bars are bent outward at the top to minimise fouling the horse's jaw near the molar teeth.

It goes without saying that this bit, like any other of any type, should always be put on the bridle so that any bending of the cheeks is to the outside *and at the top.* It is a small fault with this snaffle that, having only one half of the cheek bar bent outward, it can be put on upside down. A small fault but a real one where inexperienced people looking after a horse and gear are not supervised.

The cheek ring — the loose ring to which the rein is attached — is set outside the cheek bar. This means the joint is kept away from the horse's lips so that when wear occurs, as it must and always does, there is no possibility of the lips being pinched in the worn gap.

This setting of the cheek ring outside the cheek bars, by increasing the length, gives an increased nutcracker effect to the jointed mouthpiece. A slight but unavoidable defect.

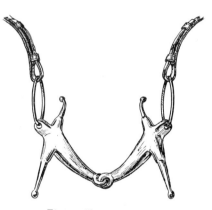

Figure 11.
The "F.M." Snaffle showing the bend in the mouthpiece and also how, like most snaffles, it drops in the centre when the cheek-bar is released. The weakest parts of the specimen shown are the rings, which are too thin and will be a weak spot when the bit is worn. We all know these days of the motor car that big bearings last longer than small ones.

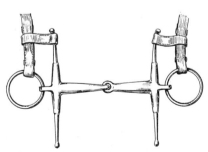

Figure 12.
The "F.M." Snaffle. A full-bar snaffle showing its reasonably thick mouthpiece and well-fitting centre joint. The upper bar is bent outward to avoid the horse's molars as much as possible. Clipped up to the headstall as shown, the centre joint does not drop in the horse's mouth. (As this snaffle can be and often is put on up-side-down, it is to be preferred if the lower cheek bar is also bent outwards.)

Centre Joint Does Not Drop

The "F.M.", like any other jointed snaffle with a full bar, can be prevented from dropping in the centre by keeping the top half of the cheek bar parallel with the bit headstall by a keeper, as illustrated (Figure 12), or by any other means that may be available. This prevents the centre joint from dropping down in the mouth.

The risk of the young horse developing the tongue over the bit habit is thus greatly lessened and the snaffle may be fitted rather lower in the mouth and so in a much more comfortable position, as a result.

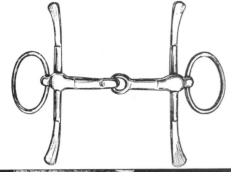

Figures 13 and 14.
A full bar snaffle frequently found on old stations. Very similar to the "F.M." The one shown in the sketch is worn out, as the centre joint shows. The cheek bar being splayed out at the top and bottom means it can be put on with either side up, and the thicker rings and larger bearing for them is another advantage. The mouthpiece could, with advantage, be thicker. Some stockmen chop off the upper cheek bar and convert it into a half bar shown in Figures 17 and 18.

Figure 15.
A Jointed Pelham. With curb hooks removed as shown a jointed pelham becomes, for all practical purposes, a Jointed Snaffle, the mouthpiece of which will not drop in the centre.
Jointed pelhams are almost invariably made too thin and sharp; a bad fault the reason for which is not clear.
See Chapter 13 for more about this bit, for it has its uses.

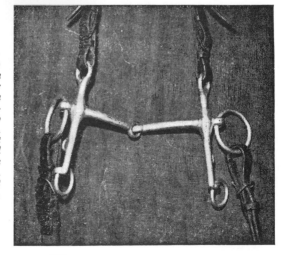

27

A horse's tongue habits, once formed, are not easily altered; and so after a suitable length of time when correct habits have been established, it will not be necessary to keep the cheek bar parallel with the line of the lips in this manner — which can be an occasional source of trouble, particularly with 3-4 year old horses.

Horses of this age and up sometimes to $4\frac{1}{2}$ years of age, are teething, often having as many as eight big molars bursting through the gum at about the same time. Young horses will occasionally fight any bit and then, although the top of the bar is bent outward slightly, it will press against the horse's cheek and gums. Any pressure by that upward-extending bar on any spot near the new teeth will make even the gentlest animal behave in a most erratic manner, to the possibly grave concern of his rider. The worst effect, however, is on the horse. The horse, if this happens with any regularity, soon becomes frightened of the pain and becomes stiff and resistant (this matter has been fully discussed in Chapter 4).

So, with horses $4\frac{1}{2}$ years of age and under, I recommend either that you do without the keeper or fit a much longer one if the horse is not going well in this bit.

Since writing the above in draft form I have had a difficult 8-year-old thoroughbred to school; he relaxed and behaved within five minutes of my releasing the top half of the cheek bar!

THE HALF-BAR SMOOTH JOINTED SNAFFLE or SPOON SNAFFLE

Figure 16.

The Half Bar Snaffle. This is among the best of the snaffles and is much favoured—in racing circles particularly. The half-bar, which should always be faced downward as shown, engages on the bottom jaw and stops the snaffle pulling through the mouth. A cheek bar that projects upward does little to prevent the bit pulling through when the horse opens his mouth.

A full bar snaffle that projects upward is not suitable for racing if only because its upward projection can become caught up in starting gates. Mrs. B. Lockwood's most successful steeplechaser, "North Alaska" and Graham Sommerville.

28

There are several other types of snaffle where the centre does not drop and these may be found more suitable, at least during the earliest months of mouthing.

"KEY" SNAFFLE OR MOUTHING BIT

Years ago quite a number of riders who had the making of a young horse's mouth used these Key or Mouthing Snaffles. They are intended to be used when the young horse is being mouthed with side reins. In this country that generally means when the horse is standing in the stockyard, bitted and saddled, with reins running from bit to girth. In most European countries this mouthing is done when the horse is moving forward on the lunge. The purpose of the "keys" is to get the horse to play with them with his tongue, the object being to keep his mouth moist and the jaw mobile and light.

This bit unfortunately sometimes has the opposite effect, and the horse finding the "keys" a nuisance, gets them to one side of his mouth and closes his lips to immobilise them. The bit itself, with or without the "keys," is a good one. There is a ring-in-the-mouth from which the keys hang and which also reduces the nutcracker action of the bit, and I have never seen a Key Snaffle that did not have a good thick mouthpiece.

The weight of the "keys" at the joint of the mouthpiece tends to drag the centre very low and so encourages the habit of getting the tongue over the bit. As the Key Snaffle is always made with a full cheek bar, it can be clipped or tied to the bit headstall in a similar manner to the F.M. Snaffle. This is not likely to affect the molars, as this snaffle is only intended for mouthing where the reins are attached to the saddle prior to the horse being ridden. It is not usually used for riding.

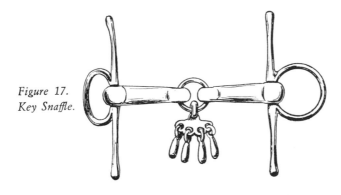

Figure 17.
Key Snaffle.

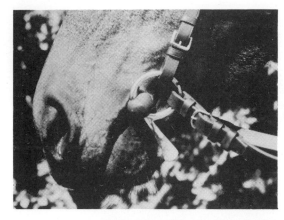

Figure 18.
*A Spoon Snaffle with
rubber covered mouthpiece
(see also Figure 29 page 35).*

RING-IN-THE-MOUTH SNAFFLES

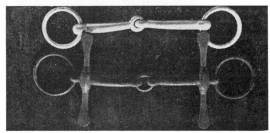

*Figure 19. A Bridoon and a Ring-in-the-Mouth Snaffle (below). It is claimed for the
ring-in-the-mouth that it has a more even bearing on the bars of the mouth and that
this type of joint outlasts the conventional type.
The one shown is a "Tom Thumb" and is well and favourably known among Australian "Old-timers." A sort of miniature "F.M." Snaffle, it has all the virtues of the latter
and it cannot be put on up-side-down.
The Ring-in-the-Mouth offsets the tendency to additional nut-cracker action resulting
from the reins being attached to the extention outside the cheek bar. A GOOD BIT;
all that I have seen seem to have a smaller mouthpiece than usual although without
doubt, makers will supply it in the usual, large, medium and small sizes.*

SPANISH SNAFFLE — A POPULAR SPECIAL BIT

This type of bit has enjoyed considerable popularity in Australia since the
visit of Mr. John Sheddon, who was invited to Melbourne about 1953.

Although called a snaffle, this bit does not really qualify to be in that
group as it is fitted with a curb chain and is capable of some slight lever
action, although very limited. On the other hand, although it has a curb

Figure 20.
*The Jointed Spanish Snaffle.
For some reason it is usually
made with too thin a
mouthpiece.*

30

chain and can operate with this limited leverage, it does not usually do so. It is generally made with three types of mouthpiece: jointed, port-mouthed and half-moon. When it is procurable, I prefer the port-mouth to either of the others but the half-moon runs it a close second.

It will be seen from a glance at the illustrations that the full length of the lower cheek is only about equal to the distance from the mouthpiece to curb-hook. The lever thus gives little or no additional power (see Chapter 10 on leverages) even if the rein could be kept at the lowest part of the cheek. As a matter of fact, it can operate from that position only when the horse's head and neck are in an overbent position and the rider's hands are held very low. Ordinarily when the reins are tight they raise the buckles to the position level with the mouthpiece and there is no lever action and certainly no power gain from leverage.

"Why do so many horses that pull on an ordinary snaffle, go well in this bit if it isn't more severe?" may well be asked.

The answer is that it is more effective because it hurts *less*. Pain makes a horse pull. In this case, the effect of the milder bit is enhanced by the fact that most riders think that because it has a curb chain it is naturally more severe, and so they tend to handle it lightly! A mild bit and a light hand help produce the desired effect.

Figure 21.
The Half Moon Spanish
Snaffle.

Much of the value of this bit (its mildness) comes from the curb chain which prevents, or at least limits, the upward movement of the bit towards the back teeth or molars. This upward movement of the ordinary snaffle is a serious defect and is described in detail in Chapters 4 and 7. If you have a serious mouth trouble with a snaffle bit and the horse "pokes his nose," then I recommend this bit for a trial as well as one or two others, such as the Half-moon Snaffle with chin strap. By stopping the upward movement of the bit, the pressure of the reins is kept in the proper and intended place.

All things considered, the Spanish Snaffle is a good bit and is deservedly popular with the show-jumping fraternity both in Australia and overseas. Its mild and constant contact with the mouth does not unduly distract the horse's attention from the job in hand, be it show-jumping or anything else.

The Jointed Spanish Snaffle is also good and might be found to suit some horses better than the port mouthpiece. Unlike the ordinary jointed snaffle, the mouthpiece does not drop in the centre and this tends to check any tendency of the horse to get the tongue over the bit. With the curb chain and hooks removed the Spanish Snaffle becomes a true snaffle, and a good one. I have said a lot about this little snaffle, for some are prejudiced against it.

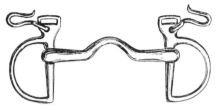

Figure 22.
The Port-mouthed Spanish Snaffle.

My discovery about port mouthpieces to which I draw your attention in Chapter 11 may well lead to the "port" being made, perhaps, up to an inch wider. Such a mouthpiece would, I feel sure, be an advantage — except for those riders who give sudden hard pulls with the rein on one side.

DOUBLE SNAFFLES AND THE "W" SNAFFLE

Double Snaffle

The use of two snaffles in the mouth at the same time is sometimes recommended to prepare the horse for a double bridle. It might be a useful practice and there appears to be nothing to be said against it provided one is fitted higher than the other. It might appear at first thought that two bits would be more severe than one. The opposite is the case. The larger the area over which the pressure is spread the less it worries the horse — but don't let this fact mislead you into buying a "W" Snaffle!

Figure 23.
The "W" snaffle. A snaffle that is not recommended. It will be seen that although it has a double mouthpiece the weight of the rider's hands is not distributed over a larger area. Its two thin cruel mouthpieces only increase the leverage action of the ordinary jointed snaffle. The "W" it forms gives the bit its name.

Figure 24
The twisted "W" snaffle—is an atrocity. More about twisted and other non-smooth mouthpieces in the next chapter.

32

A four-ringed snaffle is usually an ordinary smooth snaffle or bridoon with two additional rings placed, loose, on the inside of the ordinary cheek rings.

On driving bridles the winkers are sewn to the bit headstall and to give

Figure 25.
The Four-Ringed Snaffle doing the task for which it is designed—allowing the whole of the weight of the reins to go on to the bars of the mouth.

Figure 26.
The Four-Ringed Snaffle with the reins passed through both sets of rings, thus putting some weight on to the noseband. If the headstall is also passed through both sets of rings even more weight is placed on the noseband.

33

stability to the headstall, and to stop the winkers flopping about, the bit headstall is also passed through a loop sewn to the noseband. This idea is quite effective as far as the winkers are concerned, but it has the drawback that much of the tension on the reins usually goes on to the noseband if an ordinary bridoon is used. This can be avoided — or not — by using a four-ringed snaffle.

When the headstall is buckled to the inner rings of the four, and the reins are buckled to the outer rings only, then the whole weight on the reins goes onto the mouth (see Figure 25). On the other hand, if either the bit headstall or the reins are buckled to both rings each side, then the effect of the four-ringed snaffle is exactly the same as an ordinary bridoon (I am calling this snaffle a BRIDOON for, as the illustrations will show, the cheek rings have of necessity to be small — about the same size as the rings of a bridoon). The illustrations show exactly how they act.

Figure 27. The Four Ringed Snaffle used on a riding horse. It seems to serve no useful purpose in such a case. It might, to some extent, stop the jointed snaffle from dropping in the centre. (See Chapter 17 on "Tongue over the bit" habit.) On the other hand there is certainly nothing wrong about it.

Nose Pressures

It is a fact well in keeping with what is being consistently advocated here — the milder the bit the better — that many horses go better when a proportion of the weight on the reins is taken on the nose. The less painful the bit the better the average horse goes in it.

Quite a number of drivers who use the four-ringed snaffle, buckle the rings together because they find the horse goes better with them that way, i.e. with some pressure on the nose. If you have such a bit then you are at an advantage when DRIVING with blinkers in that you can use it in the way that best suits your horse.

Riding horses that fear the bit excessively and poke their noses out as a result, often go very much better fitted with a noseband or other device designed to take a proportion of the weight of the rider's hands.

34

The rubber snaffle is usually a little less than an inch thick and slightly half-moon shaped. Those on sale in Australia are almost invariably flexible and the rubber re-inforced with a chain centre or core.

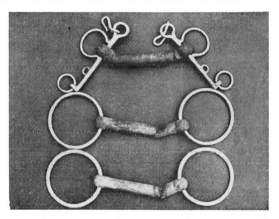

Figure 28. Flexible, soft rubber mouthpieces with chain centres. The chain, which is visible in at least one of the snaffles shown gives the necessary strength while permitting the mouthpiece to bend. These two snaffles each lasted only a few minutes before this particular horse chewed a piece out of them. The pelham (top) which tends to lock on the jaw, lasted a little longer.
A vulcanite pelham or "Mullen mouthed pelham" is a much better proposition. See Chapter 13 on pelhams.

Figure 29. Rubber covered half-bar or "spoon" snaffle (shown in use in Figure 18). This snaffle will be found useful when a horse has a bruised or over-sensitive mouth. With most horses—not all—it is a better proposition than those with a chain centre. Another variation is to cover the two halves with leather, the sewn seam, I need hardly say, being to the front of the mouthpiece.
A good bit to try with a horse that tosses and worries with the bit.

Do not confuse this SOFT rubber with the vulcanised mouthpiece, which is HARD rubber and inflexible. Shown in Figure 4 page 12.

Throughout these pages the value of a mild bit is stressed as being more effective than a sharp painful or cruel one, yet I cannot recommend this flexible bit without reserve. *Some horses and riders get on well together with it* however, and the bit is also sometimes useful for injured or super-sensitive mouths

The flexible snaffle is not suitable for horses that "lean on the bit," a type of pulling due to the horse letting the rider "carry his head for him." The soft comfort of the rubber bit tends to encourage the horse in this fault. Being flexible and of soft rubber, the mouthpiece also wraps around the lower jaw to some extent if a horse (or rider) pulls hard, and this can cause soreness and more trouble. Some horses tend to draw this type of bit up into the back teeth with their tongues, and when this happens they soon nip pieces out of the rubber and so ruin the bit.

This bit is, however, useful for horses with a lot of loose skin on the bars of the mouth which is pushed and pinched against the first molar by an ordinary snaffle. It is advisable in any case to use a running martingale and second rein with this bit (see Chapter 14, Martingales).

Mouthpieces covered with hardened rubber are much more common in pelhams (Figure 4, page 12). Any bit should, ordinarily, be mild and painless BUT should also be capable of demanding respect from the horse should he become wayward. Soft rubber does not usually comply with this last requirement; the hardened rubber does.

HALF MOON SNAFFLE WITH CHIN STRAP

Figure 30.
Half Moon Snaffle with Chin-strap. The "chin-strap" prevents the snaffle working up the jaw and fouling the molars.
This is a badly made and designed bridle and is worth comparing with the one below in Figure 32. The rounded edges of the buckles (other than the reins) break leather much more readily than do straight edges. Notice, too, the very long cheek pieces that allow for so limited adjustment: Then compare it with the shorter cheeks in Figure 32.

Half moon snaffles of any type tend to work up the jaw very readily. They are better if made like we show in Figures 30 and 31, and fitted with a strap. The "chin-strap" prevents the snaffle working up the jaw and, of course, it cannot be pulled through the mouth.

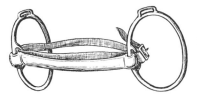

Figure 31.
The same snaffle as in
Figure 30.

Figure 32.
An ordinary smooth jointed
ring snaffle on Mrs. R.
Head's 2-year-old "Ben".
Several turns of string have
been passed from ring to
ring. This in no way
interferes but should a tussle
occur the string prevents the
snaffle pulling through the
mouth. This is especially
useful if you are compelled
to lunge a horse on a
snaffle instead of a
cavesson headstall.

GAG SNAFFLES

Comparison of different types: how they operate:
virtues and defects

The Gag is neither Snaffle, Bit nor Pelham, but as it has no curb chain and looks like a snaffle it is usually grouped with snaffle bits. The Gag is specifically prohibited in dressage competitions, but that does not mean that it is a bad bit. On the contrary it can be a most useful one.

It will be seen from Figures 33, 34, 35 and 36 that the bit headstall passes through the cheek rings and the rein is buckled, not to the cheeks, but to a ring at the end of the headstall. Any tension on the rein has a lifting effect on the bit in the mouth. It also has a tendency to make the bit revolve in the mouth and this action applies a type of leverage to the bit. The respective strengths of these two actions divide Gag Snaffles into two main groups — Ring Gags having a pronounced "pulley effect" predominating (Figures 33 and 34 page 38) and Bar Gags to which a pronounced lever effect is *added* to the pulley effect (Figures 35 and 36 page 39).

Figure 33.
Two slightly different designs
of Gag Snaffle. It is doubtful
if there is any real difference
in the effects they produce.
A lot of horses play good
polo on gag snaffles,
particularly if the rider strives
to ride on a loose rein.

Figure 34.
The additional rein permits
the use of the bit as
an ordinary ring snaffle or as
a "gag" if required.
Mrs. B. Black's "Toby."
Browband too short.

For overbent horses a Ring Gag Snaffle with its definite lifting action, in which the pulley effect predominates, is recommended.

The Ring Gag slides up the headstall much more readily than the cheek-bar type. Its pulley effect is marked, but its leverage action is very small. It is not a popular bit although some riders get on very well with it. It is disapproved because the snaffle does not slide down the bit headstall as readily as it can be drawn up; this means that it is slow to reward the horse when he yields to the rider's requirement and raises his head.

CHEEK BAR GAG SNAFFLES

Figures 35 and 36.
A full-bar "Gag" Snaffle.
Michael Scott whose horse responds extremely well to this snaffle, as do many polo ponies. Its general appearance is very similar to the "F.M." (Figures 11 and 12 page 26) but its "give" and springiness make it milder. The leverage action also takes the top of the cheek bar forward well clear of the molars, and the jointed mouthpiece will not drop in the centre. Nice loose bridle.

Badly overbent horses are often very bad pullers. Some arch and lower their heads until the chin rests on the chest and horses with this habit are very difficult to stop. The cheek-bar type of Gag Snaffle can sometimes help the rider deal with the fault.

Curb bits of any kind are worse than useless on these horses; the only real cure for such pullers is a skilful rider — one who can make it clear to the horse that it is to his own advantage to carry his head higher and to check his pace: the *rider who can encourage* at the right moment. This type of Gag Snaffle does help in this task.

Riders with such overbent horses will do well to read carefully the advice given in Chapter 1 of this book.

Bar Gag Snaffle

For the horse that "pokes his nose."

A useful bit. It will be seen from the illustrations that this type of Gag has more leverage action than the one recommended for overbent horses. It also has considerably less pulley or upward sliding action. The angle which the cheek makes with the bit headstall when the rein is tight, makes it quite difficult for the bit to slide upwards although the leverage of the cheek bar definitely lifts the mouthpiece.

FAULT TO BE OVERCOME

The most serious fault with a Gag is that it has to have a special bit-headstall made, and as allowance also has to be made for the bit to slide up and down the headstall it allows for practically no adjustment on a normal bridle, for different-sized heads.

This is quite a serious drawback and could be overcome by fixing a single adjusting buckle at the poll above the browband, instead of following the standard practice of having buckles each side of the head and below the browband.

An even better idea and one we can introduce ourselves, is to adjust the height of the bit from the lower end of the bit headstall. A slip ring or similar passed through a hole drilled or punched at the required height at the lower end of the bit headstall, below the Gag, is quite effective. Any ordinary bridle head could then be utilised for this bit. The rein would still be fastened in the usual manner to the ring provided at the end of the bit headstall.

In the meantime, if you buy a Gag bridle for a certain horse, be sure that it fits him BEFORE you buy it, as saddlers do not seem to have given this matter the thought it requires. The bridles are almost always too big and hang the snaffle too low in the horse's mouth.

Gag Snaffles, like certain types of curb bit, are particularly useful for any type of loose-rein riding such as polo and similar games and for working stock. By turning or revolving in the mouth as the rein is tightened, they cushion the effect of a violent hand. This action of a curb rein is more fully discussed in Chapter 8. A gag snaffle is effective in a similar manner.

40

GAGS AND THE TONGUE-OVER-THE-BIT HABIT

Gag Snaffles of all types are well worth trying on horses with this fault. The jointed mouthpiece does not drop in the centre and the lifting action also helps to keep the tongue underneath.

I have often noticed with a certain degree of wonder, at first, how well some horses and riders get on together when they share this bit between them — I think "share between them" is a fitting term to use, as there doesn't seem to be the slightest doubt but that the success of this bit is due more to its suiting that particular rider's hands, than to any other cause. A great many riders find their horses go well on it at polo.

Other bits also suitable for horses that poke their noses out, rush on, or reef and plunge when the rider tries to stop them, are discussed in Chapter 7 and reasons are given for the horse's conduct.

Two Reins with Gag Snaffles

Where any bit is used to correct a faulty head carriage or habit, it may be our aim to get the horse back on to an ordinary snaffle eventually, or a double bridle. The special bit is, in such cases, only a means to an end. If this is the case with a Gag, it is advisable to buckle a second rein to the ring in the usual manner (as shown in Figure 34), so that the bit may be used as an ordinary snaffle — or as a Gag — whichever suits your purpose, by merely holding the required rein a little shorter than the other.

However, if you and your horse have a job to do such as polo, polocross, hunting, campdrafting etc., then it is *how* he goes, not the shape of the bit he has in his mouth that matters. True this type of bit looks to be "an awful lot of ironmongery" to have in his mouth, but for all that it is a mild bit and if your horse goes well in it you may be sure he is finding it comfortable.

41

CHAPTER 6

THE CHOICE OF A BIT

Mouthpiece—thick or thin?: Smooth, twisted or corrugated mouthpiece?:
Mouths made sore by chafing: Correct size and fit:
Materials used in manufacture—nickel and chrome plating, stainless steel:
Solid nickel bits and stirrup irons: Worn-out snaffles

MOUTHPIECE—THICK OR THIN?

The thickness of the mouthpiece of any bit is most important. Unfortunately, many owners buy a thin bit under the mistaken impression that its lightness is a most desirable feature. Excessive weight should of course be avoided, but today, bits of all types can be procured from any reputable saddler which are both thick and light, the thicker parts being made from hollow steel.

The thinner a mouthpiece is, the more it will hurt and cut the horse's mouth. The thicker, within reason, the more comfortable the horse will find it and the better he will behave. If there should be a little additional weight, the horse with his powerful neck muscles will be quite unconscious of it.

It is possible, of course, to have a bit too thick. One inch is the very maximum that should be used, and then only on a large horse. If the bit is too thick it prevents the proper closing of the mouth and starts sores from the stretching and splitting of the lips at the corners. This tendency is greatly increased when a tight drop noseband is also used. A good mouthpiece may vary from $\frac{1}{2}''$ to $\frac{3}{4}''$ in thickness, the larger measurement being the better except for small ponies.

Bridoons are invariably much thinner. For one thing, they are designed for use on a trained horse with a second Bit on a double bridle, and there is not room in the mouth for two thick bits. Also, when the rein tension is spread on to the two bits, each will take only half the weight and so the sharpness of the bridoon is offset.

The bridoon *alone,* with its thin mouthpiece and small cheek rings, is unsuited for young horses, if only because the rings pull so easily through the mouth of a resisting horse.

Mouthpiece—Smooth or Otherwise?

It is so often said in these pages as well as elsewhere, "the mouthpiece should be smooth and not too thin," that it might not be out of place to mention some of the mouthpieces that are not smooth.

Twisted Snaffles

Figure 37. A Twisted Ring Snaffle. Twisted snaffles are terrible instruments and their use today would almost certainly lead to a prosecution for cruelty. For Twisted "W" Snaffle see Figure 24 page 32.

Fortunately these atrocities àre seldom seen now, and I am glad to say that I do not know where one could be bought in Australia today. The "twisted" snaffle has a jointed mouthpiece, each half of which is made from square-sectioned steel and each is given a twist while hot so that the sharp square edges change direction throughout its length, corkscrew fashion. These bits are terribly cruel, and cut and tear the animal's mouth brutally.

THEY ARE NOT EFFECTIVE IN STOPPING A HORSE. Twisted snaffles are much more likely to cause a horse to bolt. Their use these days would almost certainly lead to a successful prosecution for cruelty.

Corrugated Mouthpieces (including Reversible Bits)

Figure 38. A Corrugated, Straight Mouthed Snaffle—Reversible. Bits and Pelhams are still procurable today with corrugations on one side. They belong to the past and should never be purchased; even though they have one side smooth, sooner or later they are sure to be put with the wrong side to the horse's jaw. Cruel BAD bits.

These too, are seldom seen on sale today. They are too painful and cruel, and so cause the very trouble the user would avoid. They are most commonly used with port mouthpieces. The corrugations were ridges, sometimes arranged around the cannons like rings, and sometimes diagonally across the cannons. In some cases they actually were loose rings set around the cannons and could be revolved.

The fully corrugated mouthpiece (both sides) gave way to the reversible bit, one side only of which is corrugated, the other being smooth.

Although reversible bits are still obtainable, I cannot stress too strongly: "Don't buy them." Avoid painful bits. We know now that the corrugated cannons of a port mouthed bit were not as painful as was once believed, for as pointed out in Chapter 11, the cannons do not (as was thought) rest on the bars of the mouth.

Buy only bits with smooth mouthpieces, and avoid, also, those bits with THIN mouthpieces which may hurt and cut the mouth. You may be sure that if a painful bit were found to be effective in stopping a pulling horse, you would see many a horse in the hunting field and elsewhere, with a nicely fitting and brightly polished piece of stainless steel barbed-wire in his mouth as a bit!

MOUTHS MADE SORE BY CHAFING

Careful Bitting needed for "Pullers"

Pullers are more prone to mouth soreness through chafing than light-mouthed horses—their pulling naturally makes them sore. A small roughness on a bit that wouldn't affect a light-mouthed horse will soon chafe through the skin of a puller.

In the case of nickle plated bits, a sharp edge is often left when the plating begins to break away as sooner or later it always seems to do. It is this sort of trifle that so often starts a young horse on the wrong line — pulling. Once begun, the trouble often persists long after the originating bit has been discarded.

Dried saliva, if left on the bit after work, becomes very hard and rough, and is a common cause of chafing. Although I, myself, often neglect for one reason or another to attend to girths and other leatherwork when off-saddling, I invariably *wash the bit clean* before putting it away. It takes barely five seconds to do this and it is, in my opinion, the "must" in gear care. Don't let your horse's dried saliva convert the bit into a rasp. You must see that the surface of the bit is clean and *smooth* before it goes into his mouth.

Chafed Mouths

Where a bit (or anything else) is causing soreness or chafing, remove that cause immediately if at all possible. Turning the "D" snaffle or Egg-butt snaffle the other way up is often temporarily successful in this. A change of bit, even if only temporary, may be advisable until the soreness goes. In any case, the cause of the trouble should either be removed or if this is not practicable, at least kept away from the sore spot.

The big leather washers shown in the illustration Figure 10 page 25 are most effective in protecting the horse's cheeks and lips, and are useful items to keep available.

Any saddler will make them up if you cannot cut them yourself. Tape, too, adhesive or otherwise, bound over the rough edge, is often temporarily effective. Tape, however, although it may cover the roughness, tends to put even more pressure on the sore area and a "spacer" is perhaps better, i.e. something tied around the cheekpiece either above or below the edge causing the trouble, so that all pressure may be kept off the injury until it is healed.

CORRECT SIZE AND FIT—BIT, PELHAM AND SNAFFLE

No matter how carefully a bit is chosen for its type and material it will prove an unsatisfactory tool if it is not the correct size for the horse, or if incorrectly fitted.

A bit that is too large is a bad bit. By "too large" is meant its size from side to side.

A bit that might be a very mild one on a horse it fitted, becomes most painful if it can be pulled through from side to side of the mouth. Imagine a thoughtless rough hand dragging the mouthpiece and the joint of a too-large snaffle across the bars of a horse's mouth, or dragging the port of a port-mouthed pelham from side to side (try one across the bridge of your own nose some time).

A bit that is too small—too tight from side to side—also starts a lot of trouble. No matter how well it is handled it pinches the sides of the mouth after it has been on for a while, a great deal more painfully than a too-tight shoe on your own foot. The unrelieved pressure and discomfort makes the horse toss his head, and thrust his nose out. He is distracted when he is being schooled, it interferes with his jumping—and generally results in both horse and rider having a bad time. The longer the horse is ridden on any occasion with such a bit, the more it will worry him and the worse he will behave.

Whether it is too large or too small, you cannot afford to use an ill-fitting bit.

If you are compelled to use one not quite the correct size, fit a too-small bit rather lower in the mouth or a too-large one rather higher in the mouth, as the horse's head tapers toward the nostrils—and get a correctly fitting bit as soon as possible. It pays; it certainly does.

MATERIALS USED IN MANUFACTURE

Until about the turn of the century almost all bits and stirrups were made of steel or iron. Steel is strong, wears well and is not unduly heavy—but it is soon spoiled by rust unless it is kept scrupulously clean, and when not in regular use, kept oiled.

To put on and keep a bright polish on steel, a burnisher has to be used, a burnisher being a piece of bright chain mail about 4" x 5" in size, attached by its edges to a suitable sized piece of soft leather. The steel to be polished is first thoroughly cleaned and then rubbed by hand with the burnisher, sometimes for several hours, which produces a very pleasing bright polish. I think anyone who has seen a well-burnished piece of steel

45

will agree that it is much more pleasing to the eye than any stainless steel or plated steel.

Nickel Plating. World War I saw the beginning of the end of steel for bits. It just wasn't possible to keep steel bits clear from rust under the conditions existing at the Western Front. First some steel accoutrements were nickel plated, and later a mixture of metals known as "solid nickel" began to make its appearance. Solid nickel is non-rusting.

Nickel plating soon proved to be only partly satisfactory as the plating sooner or later flaked off. Nickel-plated bits can still be purchased at almost any saddler's shop. They deteriorate in appearance as soon as the plating starts to wear off, but as they are still quite serviceable their lower price assures them of a market.

Chrome Plating. If properly done, this is a much more satisfactory finish. More expensive of course, but the appearance is better and it lasts much longer. Chrome plating is generally considered satisfactory. Both chrome and nickel plating can be renewed, as bits or stirrups can be re-plated.

Stainless Steel. This is far and away the best metal used for bits and stirrups today. It is much more expensive, but is well worth the difference if one has the cash available at the right moment. It is strong, resists friction well, is rust-proof and maintains a good bright finish with very little more attention needed than a wash in clean water.

Solid Nickel Bits or Stirrup Irons. Nickel silver is a softer metal. It does not rust, but to look well it has to be polished occasionally. As the metal is weaker and softer, all bits and stirrups made of it are usually made quite heavy, and even so they wear and break after a comparatively short life. The worst feature of the metal is that, being soft, it will both bend and wear easily, and when as sometimes happens, a horse falls on the rider's leg, the nickel can bend under the animal's weight and hopelessly trap the rider's foot. Stainless steel bits and irons are well worth the extra money.

It has been said that the strength of nickel and similar metals depends upon the mixture of metals used, but if this is so, until manufacturers follow the lead of solder-makers and stamp their product to indicate its strength, I can only advise you to avoid such products for serviceability.

There are other metals and alloys used for bits and stirrup irons other than steel or stainless steel. Avoid them as being dangerous if they do not have the maker's name or trademark *permanently stamped in them.* An attached label alone should make you suspicious. The manufacturer probably wants you to forget who made it. Manufacturers who stamp their name or brand into the bit or stirrup iron want you to remember them when the article has proved its serviceability.

WORN OUT SNAFFLES

I recently visited a cattle station where they had in use several snaffles of a non-corrosive metal similar to solid nickel but called something quite different. Although there were several serviceable steel snaffle bits fifty years old and more on the station, two of those of alloy that I examined were so worn at the centre joint that we broke them both quite easily with a slight twist of the hands. They had lasted for only 20 months with constant use.

Whenever metal parts move one over the other, wear will occur. A snaffle or any other jointed bit, when it breaks, nearly always does so at the centre joint—and wear at this point is not noticed unless looked for. If a snaffle or pelham with a jointed mouthpiece has been in use for several years, it should be inspected for wear by folding the two halves to a right-angle and then giving it a twist. You may get quite a fright to find how thin a wafer of metal holds your bit together! In such a case, don't just put the bit away where it might be a danger to others; break it. It may prove to be a menace lying around where it could be used; the danger is that it *will not look worn,* for the worn part is hidden inside the joint.

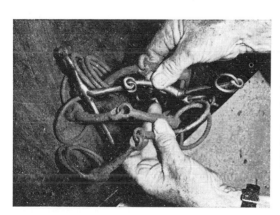

Figure 39. The top snaffle shows how a well made centre joint appears when unworn. The three lower joints show how dangerously thin the joints can wear. Such worn parts will break in the first emergency.

All types of bits wear also at the point where the cheek passes through the mouthpiece. Although this wear does not amount to a danger in steel bits as a rule, the horse's lip is frequently pinched in the gap resulting from the wear and the bit should be replaced. Some bits, are made so that the parts that wear will not come into contact with the horse's lips and these are to be preferred when buying or selecting a new bit. Freedom from pinching the horse's mouth when the bit is old and worn, is an important point and should be kept well to the front of the mind when buying any new bit.

CHAPTER 7

WHEN THE SNAFFLE IS NOT THE BEST BIT

Horses resist use of force: What happens when horse resists the snaffle:
Polo pony that "went wrong": Stress affects riding:
Correctives: A Pelham may prove best

Horses Resist Use of Force

That it is natural for a horse to resist or oppose force or pain is a fact
beyond question. Put a halter on a young horse and try to drag him forward—then notice which way he moves—or try to FORCE an untrained
horse to step backwards—or even go into a stall with a young horse (pick
a quiet one!) and try to PUSH him over to one side. It is only the exceptional animal that will not try to move in the opposite direction to that in
which you are trying to force him.

You can get a horse to do any of these things quite easily, but not by
the use of force.

And so it is with the bit, any kind of bit; try to FORCE a horse to stop,
or try to drag his nose in—and you will find that almost invariably he
will oppose you by poking his nose up and out and blunder on.

It is true of course that this "doesn't make sense"; it doesn't have to.
The horse is just behaving the way nature has made him behave. Don't
rail against it; accept it as the fact it is—something that has to be faced.
A fact that has to be dealt with.

Horses oppose force or pain until they have been taught to yield to
pressures; but even the best trained horses will revert if the force used
becomes painful enough. It is because of this tendency that bits which
can become very painful should be avoided at all times. Any bit can start
the horse resisting, but a SNAFFLE has special disadvantages because it can
become so much sharper and painful than the rider intends or often realises.

WHAT HAPPENS WHEN THE HORSE RESISTS THE BIT.

He "pokes his nose" out

When a horse's mouth is hurt by any bit, he nearly always reacts by poking
his nose up and out. With his head in this position, the reins when tight

48

draw a snaffle bit up the mouth towards the corners of the lips and towards the back teeth. (Figure 40 is typical of almost any polo scene where snaffles are used.)

If the pull on the reins continues, the cheeks and lips of the horse are then pressed inward by the nutcracker action of the jointed mouthpiece, and the inside of the cheek becomes trapped between the steel bit on the one side and the sharp edges of the first molar tooth on the other. There can be no doubt about the pain the horse is forced to bear when this happens if our hands are rough (look again at Figure 40).

Nothing could be worse than additional roughness with the bit under these circumstances, yet this is the course usually taken by the rider. Quite as often as not the roughness at this stage comes from the horse, who thrusts his head forward and out with great force and vigour.

But whether the roughness comes from the horse or from the action of the rider, the result is the same. The inside of his cheeks, crushed between the steel bit and his teeth, becomes tender and sore and eventually the lining membrane is cut, broken or torn.

Not infrequently this already bad situation is worsened for subsequent rides by grass seeds or speargrass beards having become embedded in the broken skin during feeding. Not one rider in a thousand will have any idea of the trouble that has arisen, as the injury is too high up on the inside of the cheek to be seen, and it seldom bleeds.

From this point on, the situation usually deteriorates rapidly. The horse fears a repetition of the agonising pain and at the slightest sign of the rein being tightened (certainly sometimes before the rider has become rough), he pokes his nose out in fearful anticipation. Your "nice" horse has turned into a "hard-mouthed" puller. Often the rider—thinking he has a horse with a "fool" mouth to deal with and that he may not be able to stop him —is frightened to do other than just hang on to the reins, and sometimes he gets even rougher.

Thus each provokes the other into doing the very thing each fears. By this time the pony's head is stuck right out, and the snaffle is pulling straight up the head (look again at Figure 40). All but the most inexperienced riders are fully conscious of HOW the horse behaves under these circumstances, but few seem to worry to find out "WHY."

Experienced riders know how difficult it is to control a horse once his nose is up and out, and it is to correct this that standing martingales have become almost standard usage at polo. By limiting the upward movement of the head they do tend to improve the situation—but surely, our line of action should be aimed at removing the cause of the trouble?

The only completely satisfactory solution is to give more attention to the bridle hand—but that is extremely difficult to do in an exciting situation. Even to recognise that the rider is the basic cause of the trouble is a big step in the right direction. The next should be to use a bit that will minimise the results of our shortcomings—a bit that will not work up the

Figure 40. Polo tournament at Birkalla, South Australia. It could be a game of Polo, anywhere, any time. Blue, the central figure has just missed his chance to get the ball and is making his first moves to check his pony. Note the tight rein, the "poked" nose and the tight standing martingale. Note also that the rein and bit headstall are parallel. Blue's team mate following, has checked a fraction earlier; the nose is higher, the mouth open and this snaffle also pulling up into the back teeth. The standing martingale is tightened to its limits. These are the normal reactions of a pony playing polo in a snaffle, when required to stop quickly.
All, including the Author on the right of the picture riding Mr. Bob Conroy's "Lucky", are using standing martingales, except the Umpire in the rear.

jaw is obviously a step in the right direction. Use a bit that will allow for a certain amount of error on your part—but try always to reduce the degree of that error.

A Polo Pony Began My Study of Bits

The following experience started me on the serious study of the action of bits. Started me trying to find the reasons for some bits suiting some horses while being a complete failure on others.'

The mare concerned had been a first class polo pony and had not long previously changed hands at a very high figure. In her new owner's hands she had gradually become more and more difficult to stop; then she had taken to reefing and bounding when asked to stop and generally behaving in a most desperate manner. In the end she ran away with her rider several times, and finally came to me for correction.

My experience has been that when a horse's conduct suddenly takes a change for the worse there is almost invariably a definite cause or reason for the change. In this case, with the change of riders the mild and co-operative nature of the horse had gradually disappeared and *it would seem* she had become vicious and dangerous when ridden — although I ascertained on enquiry that in stables, and when not being ridden, she maintained the same gentle character she had always had.

I suspected the bit, or the rider's handling of the bit. An ordinary examination of her mouth where the bit rested showed no injury, although there was just the slightest suggestion of pink in the saliva after playing a chukka. The first thing was to find where that pink stain in the saliva came from.

It was not until a long and painstaking examination was made with the mouth held open by a gag, that the injury was found:— on the insides of the cheeks and well above the corners of the lips — and the wound had innumerable grass seeds in it.

It was clear that the injury had been caused by the snaffle used, although it was a good smooth jointed one, of good proportions and the correct size for the pony.

This pony's case showed what can happen when the rider has been rough with a snaffle, even a good one. Even good and experienced riders, when keen and excited, are often unintentionally and unknowingly rough with their hands.

This is what had happened in this case. Ordinarily a good horseman, in the excitement of the game in which he so much wanted to excel, the new owner became unduly rough with his hands at critical moments of play. The mare had reacted in the standard manner and with her head stuck out she would open her mouth. Sooner or later the snaffle would slip up and off the front of the first molar and become jammed between the top and bottom molars where its inward pressure would force the inside of the flesh of the cheeks against the sharp projections shown in Figures 6 and 7 page 17. It was this that accounted for the injury being so very high inside the mouth.

"Running away wouldn't stop the pain" it might be thought, and that is often true (not always as some riders stop pulling from fear once the horse has become out of hand!) But a great and inescapable pain drives even reasoning humans to foolish extremes at times; how then, can we be surprised at a horse, with less reasoning power than a two-year-old child, behaving in a foolish manner? He reverts to his natural instinct and opposes the force and pain.

But to get back to the mare. Having discovered the injury and made an assessment as to its probable cause the next thing was to prevent a recurrence of the trouble, as I wanted to play her immediately if that were at all possible without making her miserable.

It was clear that the bit, whatever its type, had to be kept low and in its proper place in the mouth. It was also clear that if it did work up the mouth, any mouthpiece with a folding or nutcracker action would be the worst possible. Somehow or other I had to keep whatever bit I used off that sore spot—right away from it.

I decided I needed a bit with some sort of lever action as these clamp on the jaw and so stop the upward movement. A bit that had no joint in the mouthpiece; and if possible one that, while having a lever action, would not increase the power or severity of the rider's hands.

A bit available to me at the time was a 9th Lancer. (See Figure 45 page 69). This particular Bit had not appealed to me previously although I had noticed a lot of ponies played good polo in it. It is a mild Bit and certainly could not work up the jaw.

As one was available, I tried it—and found it worked like a charm. After a few minutes work at a walk and trot to let the mare realise she was to get a new deal, we went in to play. By the end of the chukka both the pony and I were enjoying the game.

In this case the 9th Lancer Bit "worked"—and I knew, too, how and why it worked. I began to realise that a study of the action of bits would be profitable. (I have more to say about the 9th Lancer in Chapter 13, as well as other Bits and pelhams that function in a similar manner, in that they will not work up the jaw).

Figure 41. Sinclair Hill, "Top ranking polo player in Australia" using a Mullin Mouthed Pelham together with a long standing martingale as is recommended. See also Chapters 10 and 13. Photo by courtesy of Sinclair Hill and "The Equestrian."

Stress Affects Riding

The next incident occurred a few years later and it, too, in a different way, may help to clarify this most important point.

XY was a very keen polo player, and a good horseman who took pride in breeding, breaking and schooling his own ponies.

In a very important match one day, however, he had trouble with all three of the ponies he was using. We had noticed and remarked on this in the stand as he was unmistakably showing signs of bad temper after a while, finally using both whip and bit sharply—something most unusual.

I had been watching closely and trying to assess the situation as there is always something to be learned from the unusual. After handing his horse over after the last chukka, he came to me and said. "How on earth do you explain that, T.A.? Those ponies stop, turn, twist and follow the ball beautifully and lightly when at practice, you've often watched them. Now, in an important match, they absolutely let me down. No more response than a wooden horse. Yet tomorrow, they'll go like wizards again."

The fact that they all "went wrong" at the same time seemed to indicate it was due to something he—the common factor—was doing.

This proved to be the case. The fact was that at practice he gave a good deal of attention to each pony as he rode it, and the pony was fast, smooth and easy. In an important match, however, in his keenness he was inclined to give too much attention to his game and too little to the horse under him. The ponies' mouths—and his sport—suffered in consequence.

I had learned more about bits since the occasion of the first pony so I suggested he try a Mullen-mouth (half-moon vulcanite) Pelham (See Figure 4 page 12) when playing in a match. From that time on he played them all in the pelham in matches, but did his practising in a snaffle. In other words, he recognised and made allowance for his own shortcomings in the excitement of the game and used a milder bit.

To Summarize — "Know thyself"

I certainly don't say that you cannot play good polo on a snaffle, any more than I say you cannot win a race on a double bridle, but in each case there is a better instrument available, and, if you are experiencing trouble, why not try it?

A snaffle is recommended for work where a lightly stretched rein is normally used, schooling a young horse, dressage, racing of any kind, and in some cases but not all, for show jumping.

If, for any reasons your hands are likely to become rough and jerky when riding, try something other than a snaffle. A Bit, a pelham or a hackamore. I should perhaps add here that I have never used a Hackamore or a Bit with a very long cheek-bar of the American type, so I am unable to comment on them from my own experience. But I will say that I like them both: such good results are produced with them when they are properly used. They appear only to be properly used when with a quite loose rein. The Hackamore, as it does not go into the mouth at all, is particularly valuable if the mouth is damaged or spoilt.

Recognise your own shortcomings, correct them if possible — or, as correction may be difficult, use a bit that will make allowance for them.

The expression "stretched rein" may possibly mislead a reader—it means a rein "stretched" just enough to keep the bit lightly touching the tongue or bottom jaw. In other words, "stretched rein" means "contact", light contact, with the mouth so that the horse can easily detect light *changes* of pressure.

If you are surprised that I should recommend a pelham or curb bit of any kind as milder than a snaffle read what is said in the next chapter under the heading "Pelhams and Bits can be less Severe than a Snaffle."

CHAPTER 8

WHEN TO USE A SNAFFLE
WHEN TO USE A CURB BIT

Snaffle not a perfect bit: Obedience must be enforced — deliberate resistance: Bad bit in rough hands: Pelhams and Bits can be less severe than snaffle: Loose rein compared with stretched rein

The Ordinary Snaffle is probably the bit most widely used in the world today. It is a good bit—almost certainly the best—but it is not by any means the perfect bit, nor is it suitable for all horses or all hands. Certain other types of bits suit some mouths and some hands better. These exceptions will be dealt with later. My point here is to make it clear that although a snaffle is strongly recommended as likely to be best-suited to most horses and riders, it is not always the MOST suited. Far from it indeed.

As long ago as 1857, the Austrian authority, Major F. Dwyer, wrote:

"Of all the instruments used in the handling, riding and driving of horses, the smooth common snaffle is by far the best and most generally useful. It is that by which the highest results can be obtained, while on the other hand less mischief can be done with it than with any other. The simplest form of snaffle is the best: smooth, neither too long or too thick or too curved."

Exactly one hundred years later, in 1957, Lt. Col. H. Llewellyn, Gold Medal Winner (Show Jumping) 1956 Olympic Games, wrote:

"I think that if a bit other than a really comfortable snaffle is used, great discomfort can be caused to the horse's mouth at a time when his mind and energy should be entirely concentrated in getting his four legs over an obstacle."

There can be no doubt that a snaffle is a good bit, and it should be the first we try with a young horse and for most work. But that a great many riders experience difficulties with a snaffle, on some occasions at least, is proved by the huge number of other types of bits made and sold all over the world.

Why DO so many people speak so well of the snaffle, and others find it unsuitable?

55

This depends upon both horse and rider. It is an excellent bit in good hands, but is much more severe than some curb bits when used roughly.

Obedience Must be Enforced

I repeatedly stress the fact that a mild and comfortable bit is the best bit. The more comfortable the horse when he is working, the easier he is to handle and the better the results we can get from him. But, although no trouble should be spared to keep comfortable the mouth of a willing and co-operative horse, the bit we use should also be able to enforce discipline on a rebel.

With almost every young horse there comes a time sooner or later, when, knowing what we require of him, he "plays up" and either deliberately ignores our quiet indications or actively resists them. When this type of thing occurs, it is most important that we can correctly determine the cause of the trouble. Does the horse resist just to get his own way — or does failure to understand what is wanted play any part in his opposition?

This is where experience, tact, and judgment is so important. If the rider has any doubt as to the cause of the trouble, he must give the horse the benefit of that doubt and treat it as a failure to understand clearly. If we should be wrong in taking that line, the horse will soon make it clear by his subsequent actions and we can then adopt a different course.

Deliberate Resistance. It is when the horse deliberately resists that we find it useful to have a bit in his mouth that is capable of disciplining him. The ordinary snaffle is such a bit. Although when used normally it is a mild and gentle bit, when used with any degree of roughness it can become very punishing. And this is both one of its most valuable features — and also its most serious fault.

When a snaffle is being used, even a slight vibration of one or both reins can greatly increase its severity and is usually enough to make a youngster "think again." It may be necessary to repeat this corrective action of the hand either immediately or later on, but it is seldom, if ever, that anything approaching the severity of a jerk on the mouth is warranted or necessary.

A Bad Bit in Rough Hands

Because so many riders think of the snaffle as a mild bit only, they do not hesitate to use it quite roughly in a case such as this. This is a mistake. Used roughly it becomes *extremely* painful, and when this has happened a few times the horse becomes frightened of the bit. You then have a much more serious trouble coming up.

Once he has had cause to become frightened of what the bit can do to him, the horse becomes nervous and stiff at the first movement of the rider's hands — before he is hurt. Then, instead of thinking of what is wanted of him, because he is frightened of what he thinks you are going to do to him, he becomes difficult to control. Even though he tries to do what is asked of him, his fear makes him stiff and he cannot then accomplish the task either quickly or well. You will have succeeded in making it nearly impossible for your horse to do what, relaxed, he could and would do quite easily.

So if you use the snaffle to discipline your mount, remember its latent sharpness. Use a vibration, not a jolt or a jab. Repeat the same vibration rather than increase its force if it is not at first effective, and if you should use it sharply, do so once only—or the impression may be quite different from what you hoped for. Be sure you realise that the snaffle is very sharp in its action if used roughly.

Most Pelhams and Bits Can be Less Severe than a Snaffle

A Jerk on a Curb Rein. Although a curb bit by its lever action increases the strength or force of your hands, a rough hand on a curb rein is not so severe as a rough hand on a snaffle. Few people seem to have recognised this.

When a curb rein is tightened—either gently or sharply—the end of the cheek-bar to which the rein is attached is first drawn back. It moves. Very little pressure is thus put on the bars of the mouth at first, because the cheek-bar first "gives" or revolves around the mouthpiece. It is not until later, when the curb chain has been drawn tight, that the full pressure is taken on the bars of the mouth.

It will be clear that this first giving or yielding of the cheek-bar under pressure from the rein will off-set a good deal of the punishing effect of a rough hand, as any force used will be applied to the mouth gradually or progressively.

It will also be clear that a jerk on a *snaffle* rein will be rougher and will hit the horse's jaw harder and sharper than will the same jerk on a curb rein, and that a rider who uses his hands roughly and with jerks will be kinder to his horse if he uses a curb bit. This important feature of a curb bit in comparison with the snaffle is seldom recognised. (Note that I am referring to a "rough" hand—a hand that gives jerks or jags at the mouth—not a "heavy" hand, which is not the same thing.)

Loose Rein v Stretched Rein

A snaffle is not recommended for any type of riding where a loose rein is used AND *where the task set the horse is likely to cause the rider to use the reins sharply or suddenly.*

A Loose Rein May be More Severe. When the rein is loose, the snaffle hangs slack in the horse's mouth. Any sudden pull or jerk brings it sharply in contact with the bars of the mouth. A snaffle strikes the jaw without warning if it is used sharply. On the other hand, where the rein is already stretched (in light contact) this does not happen. There is all the difference between a push and a blow.

57

We have just shown how a curb bit "breaks down" the severity of a sudden pull, and so, for loose rein riding, certain types of curb bits such as used by the American cowboys of the Western films, have much to be said for them. This is dealt with in more detail in the appropriate chapters. The point to be noted is that A LOOSE REIN ON A SNAFFLE CAN BE MORE DAMAGING THAN A STRETCHED REIN IF IT IS USED ROUGHLY, and that the "give" of the curb bit tends to offset its severity. These facts should be clearly recognised by all who ride.

It is not the rider who is rough with his hands at times who should avoid bridling his horse with a curb bit. It is the heavy-handed rider, the one who "hangs on," who does the damage with a curb bit. His clinging hand just clamps the bit on to the horse's jaw and he just "hangs on." There is nothing the unfortunate horse can do about it.

It is not the *severity* of the hold or pressure that torments the horse, even though the leverage action of the curb may magnify the hold several times. It is its continuance, plus the fact that the animal can find no way in which to escape the pressure, that so often drives a horse to desperation.

These are some of the reasons why we do not and will not always recommend a snaffle. In some hands it is much more severe than any Bit or Pelham; in other hands it is less severe. It is for us to find which suits OUR hands.

CHAPTER 9

PROGRESSIVE SCHOOLING OF THE YOUNG HORSE

The snaffle and the young horse: The horse's first lessons:
Positioning the head and neck — beware the curb bit:
Bridoon the "working" bit of a double bridle:
Teach or introduce only one new thing at a time: "Stubborn mules":
Dressage and High School riding: Bad horses.

The Snaffle and the Young Horse

My support of the snaffle finishes when the horse's mouth is hurt too much
by it—when the rider's hands become too rough. Let us before we finish
with it, look at the snaffle in the training or preparation of a normal horse
in good hands.

If you attempt to teach only a little at a time to the young horse he will
have time and opportunity to learn that little without being hurt or upset.
If, after breaking, the youngster is quietly used about the farm or station
or wherever he might be, he learns to start and stop and change direction
at the same time as he becomes accustomed to the saddle and to the rider,
under conditions with which he is familiar.

He learns these first lessons while calm, and he notices and so remem-
bers them more readily. People who only ask simple things at first seldom
have trouble, and often wonder how all these "problem horses" are created.

On the other hand, should you aim to produce a stock horse, a polo
pony, a show hack or a show-jumper, and try to get to an advanced stage
too quickly—then troubles come tumbling over one another. Often it is
not that the riders are in a hurry, they omit some of the steps in training
through not knowing the correct sequence of training—not knowing *what*
should be taught first.

When the rider asks too much and the horse does not understand
quickly, the rider often becomes more severe with the bit. If the bit hurts
the horse and he does not know what to do about it, he will become excited and "stiffen up" and may even panic somewhat. More often than not
this provokes the rider into using the bit more sharply still; and this is
where the ordinary snaffle can be a menace, as it can be so terribly painful

59

if used sharply. The more it hurts, the stiffer, the more rigid, the horse becomes.

A rough hand on a young horse is a mistake — a bad mistake. For, long after, he may instinctively stiffen or cringe in anticipation of the repetition of the pain if the bit becomes only a little sharper than usual.

The more you hurt the horse, the more you attempt, the higher you aim — the greater is the chance of disaster. One of the hall-marks of an experienced breaker or trainer is the trouble he goes to and the precautions he takes to ensure that mistakes do not occur, either with the bit or in any other matter, for the horse's memory is astonishing. Years later he may "flash back" to some unhappy early experience and repeat the happening.

Avoid, as far as you can, the circumstances that may lead to your becoming rough with the bit. I remember being told as a child:

> "One thing at a time and that done well,
> Is a very good plan — that many can tell."

This is particularly so with the training of animals. So, with the young horse, one thing at a time and "first things first."

The question is, of course: "What should be taught first?"

The Horse's First Lessons

There can be no doubt that the control of pace and direction is the first and by far the most important lesson that the young horse must learn from any bit. Although later on, for some work, we may want to control and "place" the horse's head and neck, we should not attempt to do this at first. ON NO ACCOUNT should we try to teach the horse that the bit is meant to control his pace and direction and *at the same time* try to teach him to respond to the reins by altering the position of his head and neck.

Any attempt to position the head and neck before the horse has completely mastered this first lesson and understands and responds readily by changes of pace and direction, will not only confuse him but will lead to endless troubles. It often leads to the horse becoming a "rubber-neck"— one that bends his neck this way and that, but makes no attempt to follow the direction given him. He thinks the rider requires a change of head position, not a change of direction or pace. The more the rider pulls on the rein or reins, the more the animal answers in the way he has reason to think is wanted: he arches or bends his neck. That is what the rider has taught him. Sometimes, driven to desperation by the pain of the bit that he is answering *as best he knows how,* he eventually tries something else, he may "clear out," bolt.

This is a not uncommon end-result of trying to teach too much too soon.

Teach one thing at a time. When pace and direction can be changed easily and smoothly, then tackle the next stage, but only if the horse remains relaxed while making the changes asked of him. *The condition of his muscles (relaxed) is much more important than the position of his head.*

60

Positioning the Head and Neck

Not only is the snaffle usually the most suitable bit for the first purpose we have in mind with a young horse — the essential controls — but the snaffle is also, in good hands, the most suitable bit, when the time arrives, for the placing of the head and neck — and here again, "first things first." It is only when his paces—smooth flowing paces—have been confirmed, AND NOT UNTIL THEN, should we even *think* of using the curb bit to arch the neck and to place the head at the exact angle we have in mind.

This last requirement, too, is easily taught with a snaffle by a skilful rider, but the Bit, properly used after the snaffle training has progressed sufficiently, adds elegance and refinement to the finished article.

BEWARE THE CURB BIT. The too early use of the curb bit to position the head is one of the most common causes of a difficult mouth. The Bit, the curb bit, has its place; but it is secondary and complementary to the snaffle in European-type riding and should not, ordinarily, be used until the horse responds readily to the snaffle as well as any other aids the rider may use.

Bridoon the "Working" Bit of a Double Bridle

Even when we do use a double bridle, it is the snaffle or bridoon that is the most important of the two bits used. There is practically nothing the good horseman cannot teach a horse with a snaffle. The curb bit is only an accessory to the snaffle in European-type riding — the "contact" style or the "stretched" rein.

Terms such as "on the bit," "over the bit," "behind the bit" and others, are deliberately avoided in these pages as they seem to mean different things to different people. When I get time to start the next book I have in mind (the "Why's and Wherefore's" of training and how the horse may see it!) I may have a lot to say about this "horse on the bit" condition. In the meantime note that the expression is "Horse on the bit" — not "Bit on the horse." Think it over.

Teach or Introduce only One New Thing at a Time

I have mentioned this rule here in connection with educating the horse's mouth, but this is a most important principle whatever we may teach. If *any* new lesson can be introduced in two or three parts instead of one whole, split it into those parts and teach only one part at a time.

An instance could be teaching the horse to canter with a certain leg leading. FIRST TEACH HIM TO CANTER at the correct aids or signals; do NOT try to "put him on the correct leg" at first. Teach him that the aids you use mean "Canter — NOW," and when he has that "sewn up" you can think to start and say "Now you know these aids mean canter — add this" and you emphasise the decisive aids that mean "Canter on the off (or near) lead." And that is not quite right, either, for you should NOT say "Canter, on a certain lead" — you should always put it the other way around, "On such and such a lead, CANTER." It is too late to tell him which leg you want after he has started to canter.

Try to introduce the two phases at the same time and you will almost always have trouble. Each lesson should be broken up into its parts, and each part should prepare or lead the horse into the next. So the phase that comes first can be very important. Teach the parts separately and then, when you come to combine them, you will find it surprising how quickly your horse will understand — *provided he is kept calm,* of course.

"Stubborn Mules"

The rule applies to every and all types of horses. The writer, during the first World War and when only 16 years of age, had the handling of a great many mules thrust upon him. He quickly found mules that had appeared stubborn and impossible to control, only lacked training, i.e. suitable preparation and introduction to the task required of them. They quickly, almost gratefully, responded when given the preparation and schooling normally given a young horse.

A pair of mules that had wrecked the front of a waggon by kicking at the use of a whip, quietly walked away with a similar waggon a few days later at the click of the tongue — after having been given what I now call "The go-forward lesson."

This is another instance of breaking a lesson down into smaller parts. In the "Go-forward lesson" the animal is taught that a click of the tongue means "move forward." When it is quite clear to him that when he moves forward, quietly and smoothly eventually, all irritations cease, he can be put into harness (or in these days, maybe taught to load into a float) and we will find the task simplified enormously.

The first essential to obedience is understanding, and this requires the establishment of a language of some sort or other that can be understood by both man and horse: a simple basic language. We try to get him to understand certain things mean start or go faster, *others,* stop or go slower, and *others,* change direction.

Simple as they are, these basic things have to be taught. The better you can teach, the less trouble you will have later. For all this work, you will find the snaffle the best instrument — in good hands.

Dressage and High School Riding

These, as well as ordinary showring riding, only admit the use of a snaffle and the double bridle. Well-schooled and relaxed horses in good hands, doing the work for which they have been specially trained, need no more than these. We cannot agree, however, with riders who specialise only in this type of horsemanship when they condemn all other types of bit.

I strongly recommend dressage to you as a progressive and well-thought-out and proved system of horse training and riding. Both its principles and practices can be of the greatest assistance in every type of horse-manship.

As a means to an end, dressage is invaluable, but when it becomes an end in itself it becomes a fine art—a special branch of horsemanship. Neither its saddles, its seat, its postures or its bridles are *necessarily* best for what one might call "practical, everyday horsemanship."

The fact that all who would practice dressage are not experts at it, often damages its picture. It is not my intention to damage it further—the opposite, indeed. But the dressage expert who thinks he would not have to adapt himself if he entered other types of horsemanship is not likely to fill the leading place.

Where the task in hand is such that you can give only a part of your attention to your horse, such as stock work, sports of all kinds, etc., a double bridle is certainly not the most suitable. It is for this reason that it is seldom, if ever, used. It requires too much attention, and a too accurate adjustment and use of the reins, to be practical.

A pelham is not such a delicate instrument. It is much more tolerant when used roughly. It hurts the horse less. It allows more for inconsistencies and mistakes in handling the reins, and so upsets and excites the horse less.

Bad Horses

I have made a speciality of the re-education of apparently vicious and sometimes unmanageable horses: rearers, jibbers, refusers, bounders, bolters, highly excitable animals, etc., and I have had a considerable amount of success in that direction.

Before dealing with curb bits I would like to stress that almost without exception the line taken with such horses has been first to place them on a mild thick snaffle, usually with double reins on to one of which is fitted a long running martingale. Later, after finding the basic trouble, a special bit is sometimes found to help. Often found; but first, and whenever there is any doubt, I use a thick mild snaffle.

Then, don't ride your horse as though into battle. Give him some quiet education; give him a chance to understand you and get to know what you mean. Give him a chance to avoid trouble—"Give him a go."

Use a snaffle first unless on examination of his mouth you find some injury or mal-formation. Give him every chance until he understands; usually when he does understand, sooner or later it becomes necessary to discipline him. When you are sure it is necessary—THEN YOU DO IT. Try not to lose your temper, for it is most essential that the moment he starts to behave again you treat him like an angel! Besides giving him all the discouragement you can when he misbehaves, it is EVEN MORE IMPORTANT that you give him every encouragement TO behave.

Now about curb bits, which include pelhams, for they are often to be preferred to a snaffle.

CHAPTER 10

LENGTH, PROPORTION AND SHAPE OF THE CHEEK-BAR OF ANY CURB BIT

Leverage action of curb bit: Factors affecting desirable length of
cheek-bar: Shape of cheek-bar varies its severity:
How curb chain can cause pinching: Preventing the curb chain pinching:
Turn-cheek and sliding mouthed bits: Reversible bits and pelhams

The cheek-bar, that part visible and outside the mouth, is an important part of a curb bit as it is the cheek-bar acting as a lever that makes the great difference between a Snaffle and a Bit.

Cheek-bars are made in a great variety of shapes and lengths and it is quite out of the question to review them all. It will be found of more value to understand the general principles on which they work. We can then make our own assessment of the purpose and value of any particular design we may encounter.

As with any lever the effectiveness of the cheek-bar will be affected by its length and proportions. It will be found that there are also advantages and disadvantages in certain *shapes* of the cheek-bar. Some shapes will reduce the effectiveness, severity or sharpness of the Bit.

Leverage Action of Curb Bit

If you wish to use an ordinary crowbar as a lever to prize a stump from the ground you will first place near the stump a block of wood or something similar on which the bar can operate and work. This block of wood is called a "fulcrum." The closer the fulcrum is to the weight to be lifted the less the effort or power needed to lift it. In other words, the lifting power of the crowbar will vary with the proportions of its length each side of the fulcrum.

The total length of the bar, then, may not be so important as the proportions each side of the fulcrum, i.e. two to one, or three (or more) to one.

So it is with the cheek-bar of a curb bit. A curb bit with an upper cheek of 3″ above the mouthpiece and a lower cheek of 6″ below the mouthpiece will be no more powerful than one with 2″ above and 4″ below. In each case the proportion is 2:1. We will see later, however, that *there are good reasons why the upper cheek of a Bit should not be anything like 3″ long.*

For many years now the proportion of 2:1 has been accepted as being about the most suitable for a Bit used with a double bridle. (And note that I say "about" in all these matters, as slight variations will be more effective with certain horses, mouths or hands.)

Factors Affecting Desirable Length of Cheek-Bar

The ideal overall length of the cheek-bar for a double bridle is almost universally accepted today as being approximately 5½″. This length is determined by accepting 1¾″ as the most desirable length for the upper cheek for the average horse. So, with a lower cheek of about twice the length of the upper, we have a total length of some 5½″.

Why should the Length of the Upper Cheek Bar be so Important? We find that should the length of the upper cheek be much shorter than 1½″,

Figure 42.
"The Bit falls through."
i.e.—the curb chain is a little too loose and so has permitted the cheek-bar to pull back into prolongation of the line of the rein. The curb thus loses most of its effectiveness. (See Chapter 12.) With a double bridle, however, this will not cause the pinching of the lips described later in this chapter.
The Author—who had personally fitted the curb chain—on Miss D. Mansom's "Elkedra" after winning an "educated horse" test. Elkedra, in his year, also won the Alice Springs Cup— (Racing).

65

the top of the bar to which the curb chain is attached, will have insufficient movement to operate the curb effectively unless the curb chain is most carefully and accurately adjusted for length each time it is used.

With a very short upper cheek, if the curb chain is adjusted the smallest fraction too long, the Bit will "fall through"—a term used to indicate that the cheek-bar has been drawn back to its fullest extent and has become a prolongation of the line of the rein. When this happens all leverage action is lost and the Bit then produces much the same effect as would a snaffle (see Figure 42 page 65). On the other hand if the curb is adjusted too tightly, it will be pressing constantly on the back of the jaw, and it becomes impossible for the horse to escape from its irritating effects. It will always be in action to some extent—a state of affairs that almost invariably leads to mouth and head troubles. In Chapter 12 which deals with curb chains, you will find additional good reasons for not having a curb chain too tight.

If the upper cheek is as long as even 2" it sometimes reaches too far up the head and in addition to pressing against the horse's cheeks at the molars, it causes the curb chain to ride too high at the back of the jaw.

This means that the chain will rest on the sharp branches of the jaw instead of in the smooth and rounded chin groove just below where the two branches of the jaw meet (see Figure 58 page 86).

Experience has proved that, provided the upper cheek is given a slight cant outwards, 1¾" is a good length for the upper cheek and 5½" a suitable length for the whole cheek-bar. However, if the upper cheek is *not* bent outwards as recommended, even 1¾" may be too long for the upper cheek bar; 1¼" or 1½" would be better with the overall length reduced in proportion.

Should the upper cheek of the Bit you are already using be more than 1½" in length and not bent as recommended, put it in a vice and give it a decided bend outwards—your horse will go all the better for it.

To Sum Up

The proportion recommended for the lower cheek-bar in relation to the upper bar is about 2:1.

The length of the upper cheek-bar is recommended to be about 1¾" for a double bridle, for if less than this the curb chain is very difficult to adjust so that it remains effective. If longer than 1¾" the bar tends to cause trouble by extending up to and interfering with the molar teeth, and also by tending to seat the curb chain too high on the back of the jaw.

Shape of the Cheek-Bar

It has been shown that the proportion of the lower cheek in relation to the upper cheek bar affects the power or severity of any curb bit. The *shape* of the cheek-bar also affects its severity or sharpness *but this* is *usually not recognised.*

The American Cowboy Bits, for instance, are as a rule comparatively long and so are often considered to be very severe. This is not necessarily the case however, as these Bits are almost always "back-swept," by which I mean that the lower cheek-bar is bent backwards to a considerable degree. The more the cheek of any curb bit is back-swept the less severe it can become, for, remember, full effectiveness is only obtained from any lever when the power used is applied at right angles to the lever. The more the lower cheek-bar is bent to the rear the less it can be drawn to the rear. In short, with Bits of this shape, leverage cannot be applied at the most effective angle, 90°. If, for instance, the lower cheek should be back-swept to 90°, the rein would not be able to operate the curb chain at all (see Chapter 12 on Fitting the Curb Chain).

Figure 43.
An American type of Bit improvised from an old bit with very long cheeks by Mr. Jim Munro. It can clearly be seen that the bends in the cheek-bar will prevent the curb chain and mouthpiece becoming close enough to pinch the lips at any time. An excellent padded strap has been substituted for a curb chain and hooks. The Bits shown in Figures 43 and 45 are designed for loose rein riding, as also is a "Hackamore". They are trouble-makers if the rider "hangs on". The rider must ease his hands immediately after use. A curb bit is not recommended for a horse or rider that "hangs on". i.e., one that keeps a continuous hold or pull on the reins.

When a Bit is bent back at the bottom as these Cowboy Bits often are, the proportions of lower cheek to upper cheek can be safely increased to three or four to one without increasing the power of the rider's hands, or, if you prefer it, without increasing the severity of the Bit—and this is the usual practice.

The severity of some Bits is affected in a somewhat similar way by setting the lower cheek-bar to the rear of the alignment of the top cheek-bar.

Figure 44.
The Author schooling a horse over hurdles using a Military Pelham, the active duty bit of the South Australian Mounted Police. Both reins in action with the curb chain just tight and the bottom rein and cheek-bar making an angle of 90° the bit in no way interfering with or distracting the horse.

It is all a matter of angles and this too will be broached again when we deal with the fitting of curb chains.

So, quite apart from anything else, the severity of a curb bit may be considerably affected by the shape of the cheek bars. The Military Pelham shown in Figure 44 and Figure 70 page 96 would certainly be more severe if the whole cheek was on the same alignment.

Other advantages resulting from displacing the lower cheek-bar to the rear include that, when standing idle, the horse cannot take either the rein or the cheek of the Bit into his mouth quite so easily. Bits of this and similar design also will not pull through the mouth so easily in a tussle.

To Sum Up

If the cheek-bar of any curb bit is shaped, bent or curved so that either the curb hook or the curb rein attachment (or both) is to the rear of the mouthpiece, then the movement of the cheek-bar and the tightening of the curb chain will be limited, and the effectiveness or sharpness of the curb reduced.

A great advantage in the cheek-bar being so shaped is that it prevents the pinching of the horse's lips between the curb chain and the mouthpiece, next to be dealt with.

HOW THE CURB CHAIN CAN CAUSE PINCHING

Any curb bit or any pelham having a straight cheek-bar can cause pinching of the horse's lips when the curb chain is fitted too loosely. As this pinching never occurs when the Bit used forms part of a double bridle, it may be useful to know why and how this happens.

68

Where the cheek-bar of any Bit is straight, i.e. not back-swept or bent to the rear in any way, the curb hook, the mouthpiece and the curb rein dee are all in the same alignment. When the curb chain is fitted too loosely with this type of cheek-bar, the bottom of the cheek-bar can be drawn back so far that the curb chain and the cheek-bar become parallel and touching (see Figure 45 and Figure 68 page 94).

Figure 45.

A 9th Lancer Bit fitted with special chain guard. The chain guard is extended past the mouthpiece to prevent pinching of the lips between chain and mouthpiece, when, as in this Figure, the chain is adjusted too long. Any piece of leather can be used to make the guard; the chain being passed through double slots cut in suitable places.

When this occurs, the skin at the corners of the horse's lips can become trapped between the chain and the mouthpiece as in Figure 46 page 70. As the pull on the rein increases so the curb chain and the mouthpiece grip the flesh between them, and the startled animal usually gives a leap or bound that causes the rider to hang on to the reins even more strongly. Not infrequently the skin is split and the flesh on the outside of the horse's lips crushed. But long before there is an injury like this—severe enough to draw blood that will be noticed—the horse can be having a very bad time of it without the rider having the slightest idea of what is happening.

Once the skin is damaged some swelling occurs, and the then projecting area becomes even more vulnerable to a repetition of the pinching on a, by now, very sore spot.

Trouble may now be coming up—fast. If the pinching is allowed to happen several times, the horse will begin to anticipate it and after a while will behave in the same desperate manner as described in Chapter 7, leaping and bounding as, or even before, the rein tightens and perhaps eventually bolting if the pain continues long enough.

This type of injury can only occur if the curb chain is fitted too long, and if the design of the Bit is also such as to allow the chain and the mouthpiece to come together—i.e. when the Bit "falls through."

THE CHEEK-BAR CAN BE SHAPED TO AVOID THE POSSIBILITY OF THIS PINCHING.

Several Bits and Pelhams are available today especially designed to prevent the curb chain approaching too close to the mouthpiece, even when the chain is adjusted too long. Some, such as the Smith and Brehans Pelham, the Three-in-One Pelham, etc., shown in Chapter 13, and others, *displace the curb hooks to the rear* of the alignment of the other two factors.

Figure 46.
Miss Raelene Rankine demonstrating how the loose curbchain can trap the edges of the lips—and feeling sorry for her horse.

Others, such as the Military Pelham and the American Bits just mentioned, *displace the curb rein dee to the rear* and at least one, the Scamperdale (Figure 67 page 93), *displaces the mouthpiece to the front.* No doubt there are others designed to achieve the same purpose. Which type you select might depend upon the horse's jaw, the type of work you have in mind, and, perhaps, how you yourself use the reins.

I have said earlier that this type of injury cannot occur when a bridoon is used in conjunction with a Bit, i.e. when a double bridle is used, for with a double bridle the bridoon acts as a "spacer" and keeps the skin clear of the parts that can pinch (see Figure 75 page 103). This is at least *one* reason why a double bridle is sometimes preferred, although often the rider only knows he has a trouble with a pelham that he doesn't have with a double bridle. He may not know what the actual trouble is — he just blames the pelham.

Preventing the Curb Chain Pinching

First remember this type of injury only occurs when the curb chain is fitted too loosely. Follow the instruction given for Fitting the Curb Chain in Chapter 12 and the trouble will not occur, no matter what type of curb bit you use.

This pinching can be easily prevented too, by placing anything between the skin and the bit to keep the bit away from the skin. Leather washers as shown in Figure 10 page 25 are quite effective and may be cut in several designs. I personally prefer the long chain guard shown in Figure 45. I find it easy to make, convenient to use and completely effective. The guard must be longer than is usual — long enough to extend well past the mouthpiece on either side, and it should not be less than 1¼" wide.

Another preventative is to pass the curb chain through the snaffle rein rings of the pelham as shown in Figure 47. This, too, is quite effective, but not so neat in appearance.

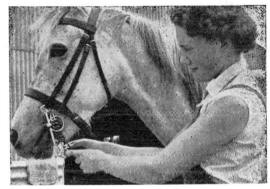

Figure 47.
Raelene Rankine shows how passing the chain through the cheek rings will keep the chain away from the lips and so prevent pinching. Read Chapter 10 for alternative action.

Pinching will not occur with a pelham if either a "Two-to-One" rein or a "link rein" is used (see Figures 48 and 49). The cheek-bar will not be drawn back far enough with either of these to cause the injury.

TURNCHEEK AND SLIDING MOUTHED BITS

Some very strong opinions are held on the advantages and disadvantages of "turncheek" and sliding mouthed bits compared with a fixed cheek-bar. As in so many controversial matters connected with horses, none is completely right—best or most advantageous—in every circumstance.

When a cheek-bar is wide as in Figure 50, some movement at the place where the bar joins the mouthpiece is a decided advantage. It allows the wide cheek to follow or conform to some degree to the shape of the horse's head. It makes for the comfort of the horse and so produces better results.

Figure 48.
The "Two to one" rein.

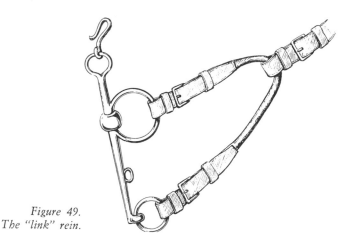

Figure 49.
The "link" rein.

When a Bit is big and heavy, there is always some advantage if the mouthpiece can slide up and down the cheek-bar for a distance of half an inch, more or less. It allows the horse to move the mouthpiece with his tongue, whereas were it fixed, the whole bit might be too heavy. The movement tends to keep the mouth fresh and light. See Figure 50.

It can be seen, then, that it adds to the horse's comfort if a wide cheek-bar can turn a little and there is also an advantage if the mouthpiece of a heavy Bit can be moved a little, independent of the cheek-bars. Most wide cheek-bars are therefore moveable, either turn-cheek or sliding, or both.

The Weymouth type Bit. There seems to be no such advantage, however, with the Bits usually used in a double bridle, which are light enough for the horse to move easily with his tongue and which seldom have cheeks more than ½″ wide. On the contrary, there are some distinct, though slight, advantages in bits such as the Weymouth having the cheeks fixed to the mouthpiece.

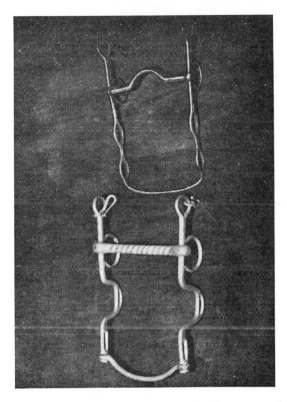

Figure 50. Pelhams of the past. Both poorly designed and unnecessarily long although their proportions, i.e.—lower cheek to upper—are about the recommended 2 to 1.

TOP. *This non-reversible, fixed cheek pelham has an unusually large "port" about which, after you have read Chapter 11, you may reserve your opinion. Everything we have been taught about ports we have to reconsider and one of an unusual width may, possibly, prove to be useful. The upper cheek which is 3 ins. long, should be bent sharply outwards and away from the cheeks of the horse. A poorly designed bit.—BAD.*

BOTTOM. *Being reversible, the upper cheeks of this pelham had to be left straight. A badly designed bit, for while the mouthpiece is left straight, which makes for mildness, the corrugated side presented to the mouth when reversed, provides for maximum sharpness or severity.*

In both cases as the cheeks project well below the horse's muzzle they could easily become trapped in appertures or on the reins of other animals were the ends not bridged.

On any bit, whether the upper cheek be long or short, it can safely be given a decided cant outwards when the cheek is fixed — whereas when a

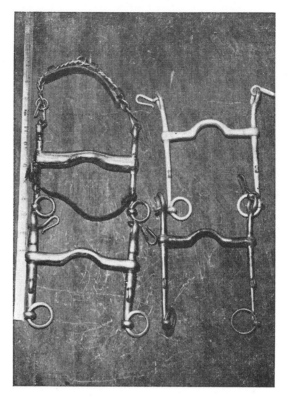

Figure 51. Four types of Bit. All designed for use as part of a double bridle.

Right top and bottom. Two port mouthed, fixed cheek, non-reversible Bits. Length of each, 7 ins. Proportions of lower to upper cheek approximately 2 to 1. The upper cheek well thrown out in each case. Thickness of cannons, ½ an inch.

Top left. The Ultra Modern Bit—Fixed cheek; length 5-1/4 inches. Cannons 7/8 inch thick. (Thicker than is necessary for a double bridle?) Port just high enough to keep the bit centred and the mouthpiece of tubular stainless steel. With such short upper cheeks an outward cant is not necessary although it could be an advantage in some hands and in any case could do no harm.

But note how the points of the curb hooks are bent away from the horse, and, as you may see in later pictures, upside down by normal standards. More about the curb hook in Chapter 12. (Fig. 57 page 85).

Bottom left. Smooth, sliding, port mouthed, Bit. Cannons 5/8 inch thick. Cheeks 6 inches long with the inner side of the cheek bar flattened so as not to pinch the horse's lip when it slides up and down. Obviously it is not made to be reversible but it can be used in the reversed position—in which case pinching may occur. Shown also in Figure 55 page 79.

None of these Bits are suitable for use other than in conjunction with a bridoon— as part of a double bridle.

cheek-bar can be turned right around, the outside can become the inside of the cheek. In this case it should be made short and left straight, for if it is long and bent to the outside there is always the danger of it being put on the wrong way around.

There is one type of sliding-mouthed bit that *appears* to be reversible but it is not. When put on correctly there is a flat surface on the inside to the horse's lips, preventing pinching when the mouthpiece slides up and down; when reversed the side then turned inwards can pinch horribly. These non-reversible Bits are OFTEN PUT ON THE WRONG SIDE INWARDS and it would be a great advantage if the manufacturers could stamp the word "Front" on the front of the mouthpiece (see Figure 51 page 74 and also Figure 55 page 79). It is a certainty that many purchasers would appreciate it. There is little if anything, to be said for a reversible bit.

To Sum Up

If you are still doubtful as to which is best for the Bit of your double bridle, the following points may influence your decision: the Fixed Cheek is usually cheaper to buy; it lasts longer, as there are no moving parts to wear; and it is quieter.

Only in the bigger and heavier Bits or Pelhams is the advantage of movement clear beyond doubt.

CHAPTER 11

THE PORT-MOUTHED BIT
The Theories of Centuries Proved Wrong

Description: The Old Belief: A New Era in Bitting:
Tongue Still Acts as Cushion: Bit is Kept Centred:
What Difference will New Knowledge Make: A "Port" is a Kind of
Half-moon Mouthpiece.

The "Port"

The names of all the parts of a bit have been given on the pages preceding Chapter 1. You will see there that a "port" is an upward curve in the centre of a mouthpiece. The two horizontal parts each side of this curve are known as "cannons".

In this chapter I am going to challenge — not the indisputable fact that a port mouth has advantages over a straight mouthpiece — but the long-held ideas as to what these advantages are: ideas that have been taught for centuries and that now prove to be wrong.

For hundreds of years it has been claimed that the advantages of the port mouthpiece were due to its increasing the severity of the bit. This theory seems to have been universally accepted and I know of no horseman or writer who has questioned the truth of the statement. This is surprising, as it is well established nowadays that a severe bit is less effective than a milder one.

Before concluding this book, therefore, I decided I should try to find for myself the reason for this single exception. *I find that there is no exception.* Contrary to all that has been said and that you, like myself, have probably repeated, the advantages of the Port are due to its BEING MILDER IN ACTION, not sharper.

The Old Belief

The theory is held that with a straight mouthpiece the tongue relieves the bars of the mouth (the jaw bone) of the pressure of the Bit as shown in sketch Figure 52 page 77. This is so, but the theory goes further.

The port, it is claimed, allows the tongue to slip or fit into the curve and the cannons of the mouthpiece are then allowed to drop and *press upon the more sensitive bars of the mouth* as shown in sketch Figure 53. *This it does NOT do.*

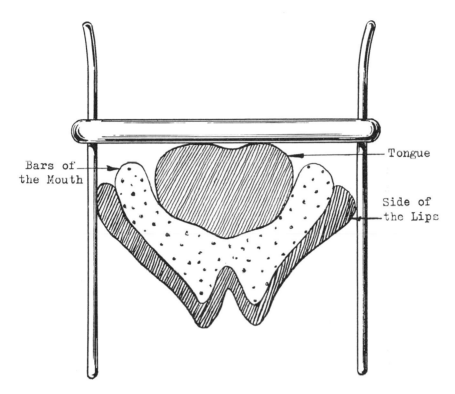

Figure 52. *"Section of the horse's jaw showing how the tongue can relieve the bars of the mouth of pressure if the bit has a straight mouthpiece." The quotation is correct but the sketch is incorrect. No horse ever had a jaw as wide as this.*

I find that if the port is narrow enough to allow the cannons to rest upon the bars of the mouth, then it is too narrow for the tongue to fit inside the port.

If the port is wide enough to allow the tongue to fit inside it, the jaw is so narrow at this spot that the bars are ALSO within or under the port, depending on its height.

That such fallacious thinking has gone on for centuries is hardly conceivable. The very ease with which it can be disproved seems to have protected it. Thousands like myself have realised that, were it right as we accepted it to be, the jaw was so narrow that the slightest movement of the mouthpiece to one side would compel one cannon to drop off one bar.

The sketches reproduced in Figures 52 and 53 are taken from a British Army handbook dated 1937, a reproduction itself from earlier handbooks. A U.S. Military handbook dated 1950 that I have here before me also fully supports the theory in its text.

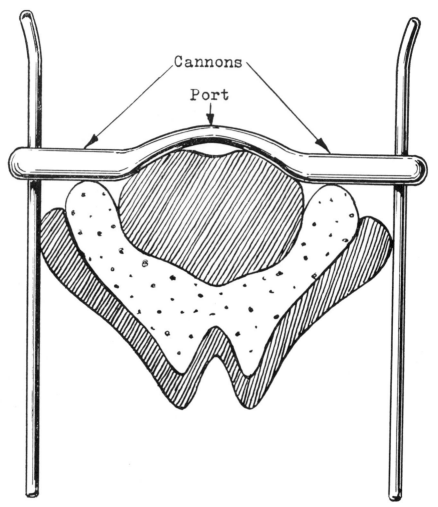

Figure 53. "Showing how the tongue fits into the "port" thus allowing the "cannons" to press on the bars of the mouth. A port-mouthed bit is always more severe—more sharp—than a straight or halfmoon." Both the quotation and the portrayal of the horse's jaw, in fact, are incorrect.

Compare these drawings of an *imaginary mouth* — particularly the jawbone — with the photographs of the jaws of two big 16 h.h. horses shown in Figures 54 and 55.

One glance at the photographs disposes of the claim that the port allows the cannons to drop on to the bars of the mouth. Neither the old sketches nor the old theory are based on fact.

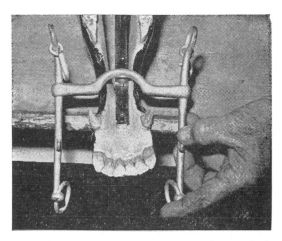

Figure 54. This is the photograph of the bottom jaw of a big steeplechaser. A big horse. It clearly proves that the "port" does not allow the "cannons" to drop on to the bars of the mouth. The jaw is much too narrow for this to happen. The port centres the bit in the mouth; keeps the tongue above the bars of the mouth so as to act as a cushion and thus makes the bit milder.

Black paint has been applied to the outside of the jawbone and the line where black and white meet is the actual "bar" of the mouth. In this case, as in many others—as thin and sharp as the back of a knife. Note, while you have the photo in front of you, that the first molar tapers to quite a sharp edge.

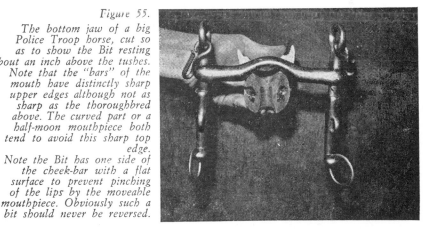

Figure 55.

The bottom jaw of a big Police Troop horse, cut so as to show the Bit resting about an inch above the tushes. Note that the "bars" of the mouth have distinctly sharp upper edges although not as sharp as the thoroughbred above. The curved part or a half-moon mouthpiece both tend to avoid this sharp top edge.

Note the Bit has one side of the cheek-bar with a flat surface to prevent pinching of the lips by the moveable mouthpiece. Obviously such a bit should never be reversed.

How can an error so gross and so easily detected have been so universally accepted?

A NEW ERA IN BITTING

The Tongue Still Acts as a Cushion

Before we go on to study what actually does happen, let me point out that the port does not allow the tongue to drop inside until the bottom of the cheek bar is drawn back. As long as the curb is loose the port lies on top of the tongue as does a straight mouthpiece.

It has always been stated or claimed that the port, by giving freedom to the tongue, prevented the tongue acting as a cushion and allowed the bit to drop on to the sensitive bone of the jaw. A glance at either of the photographs shows that with a port not only is the pressure still taken mostly on the tongue but that the tongue *is kept* in that position in the centre, where it acts as a "cushion" to the bars of the mouth around which the port curves. This is not all, for instead of giving freedom to the tongue, the port tends to imprison it.

Look again at the photographs and compare them with the sketches. Notice that the top or bearing surface of the bars of the mouth is not the nicely rounded curve shown in the sketches, Figures 52 and 53, but that in actual fact it has quite a sharp ridge along the top. In one jaw I examined the ridge was as sharp as the back of a dinner knife. Direct pressure on that edge — with steel resting on bone — would be painful. Think of the effect of a very rough hand!

Every jaw I have examined (and I mean the jawbone of a dead horse that you can actually see and feel!) *has had such a ridge of varying degree of sharpness.*

Look again now at the photographs and see how the rounded port — or even a half-moon mouthpiece — tends to transfer pressure away from the sharp ridges on to the sides, where it is much less painful.

Bit is Kept Centred

As the curb rein is tightened, and not until then, the port starts to encircle the tongue and the bottom jaw. In Chapter 12 following, reasons are given why the cheek-bars should not be drawn back to make an angle of more than 45° with the line of the jaw. This being so, the port will never be at the right angle shown in Figures 53 and 55 unless the chain is too loose; loose enough to allow the bit to "fall through." Which means it is ineffective.

This curving of the port around the bottom jaw as the rein tightens, we now find, most effectively *keeps the Bit centred in the mouth* — the jaw lies IN the port — and among other advantages this "centering" keeps the upper cheek-bar away from the molar teeth, a very great advantage in my opinion.

As the bit rein tightens, the Bit begins to revolve: not on or around *the cannons* as we have thought, but around *the port*. This is an important

80

fact — not in keeping with the old ideas. It means that a high port will not necessarily move upwards towards the roof of the mouth as the mouthpiece of the Bit is revolved. It can, according to its width and height, do the opposite and allow the cannons to drop even further. This in turn can affect the leverage effect of the cheeks.

What Difference Will New Knowledge Make?

That we will need to re-adjust our thinking on straight, half moon and port mouthpieces is certain, but what will result from the re-adjustment is by no means certain and will need many years of checking. The really important fact is that a port mouthpiece makes the Bit milder and less punishing *in many ways,* and that all the advantages and perhaps more — also extend to the Pelham. The facts are as they have always been; it is our knowledge and our theories which have been in error.

A Port is a Kind of Half-moon Mouthpiece

I have for many years favoured and recommended a half-moon mouthpiece for a pelham, sometimes in preference to a port mouth. Now I find that a port is a sort of half-moon mouthpiece — a short one — into which the jaw drops and in which the rein and the curb chain hold it secure. Perhaps a slightly wider port would suit some of the horses that now go better in a half-moon.

When the fact that the jaw drops into the port is accepted, we might find wider DEEPER (not higher) ports beginning to appear. In the meantime, let me recommend a half-moon mouthpiece or a port mouthpiece used with a correctly adjusted curb chain.

One thing about mouthpieces I have found inexplicable. The bend in a half-moon mouthpiece is made in a different direction from the bend in a port. In the latter the bend is made upward, towards the top of the cheek-bar; in the half-moon it is bent forward at right angles to the cheeks. I cannot remember ever having seen either a Bit or a pelham that did not conform to these differences. Perhaps I shall hear from someone who knows why the difference is made. It could be that the ideal angle is midway between the two — I can see good reasons for the direction in which the port is shaped, but none at all for the half-moon. Yet they are all made that way.

(We now find one type of Bit from Germany is designed that way. This is the Bit with the curb hooks reversed. See Figures 51 page 74 and 57 page 85.)

CHAPTER 12

CURB CHAINS AND HOOKS AND
THEIR CONSTRUCTION

Why Double Links, Wide-centre Chains: Protected or Padded
Curb Chains: Adjusting the Curb Hook

FITTING THE CURB BIT AND CURB CHAIN

Height of the Bit and Position of Curb Chain: Fitting the Curb Chain:
Fitting Link: How Long or Tight should the Curb Chain be:
Fitting of Curb Chain on Double Bridle: To Sum Up:
Old Military Instructions

Examine your curb chain and you will probably find that except for three links at each end the chain is double-linked, i.e. each link has two others linked through it, not one. You will also notice that each link has a peculiar kink, so that if you take hold of one end of the chain and twist it clockwise, it will gradually flatten out and take on the flat appearance of a strap.

The aim of the designers is to provide a smooth flexible flat surface to come into contact with the back of the horse's jaw. Just as a thick mouthpiece hurts less because the pull is spread over a larger surface, so too, the double-linked chain is less painful, because it doubles the points of contact or pressure and so halves any resultant pressure or discomfort. Like all bits, the modern curb chain, too, is milder than those of the past

The single links at each end of the chain are for adjustment purposes to keep the double-linked section in a central position, as only the centre of the chain presses on the horse's jaw.

The first chains were single linked, as shown in (1) and (2) of Figure 56. These were at first permanently fixed to the off-side of the Bit as in (9) of Figure 56, and all adjustments had of necessity to be made on the near side. With the object of increasing the area of contact and thus making the curb chain milder in its action, bit-makers then produced an improved "wide-centre" chain of the type shown in (2), (3) and (4) of Figure 56.

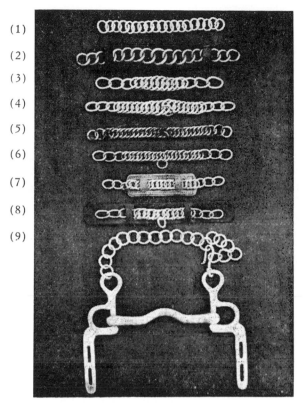

(1)

(2)

(3)

(4)

(5)

(6)

(7)

(8)

(9)

Figure 56. Curb Chains

No. 9 (on the bit) shows the original single links, each link being more or less round.
No. 2 followed: a single link still but with enlarged links in the centre. The theory
was that a larger area of contact would worry the horse less. See also Figure 46 page 70.
No. 1 was a further improvement. All single links still but slightly oval in shape. Very
cleverly designed; this chain which has the same number of links—19—as that on the
military pelham shown at 9, and is also the same length before twisting, becomes
a good 3 ins. shorter when twisted correctly. This gives a good deal more skin contact
than the circular type link.

The chains shown in 3-4-5-6-7 and 8 followed, all being double linked in the centre
but with three single links at either end for adjustment purposes.

The overall length of the chains vary and so do the lengths of the adjusting links at
each end. No. 8 for instance has a much greater range of adjustment than has 5. This
I would say, is a slight advantage.

Nos. 7 and 8 show chain guards. No. 7 being padded and being the bare length of the
double linked section.

No. 8 is the type of chain guard I referred to in Figure 45 page 69, plain stiffish
leather with a couple of slots cut to permit the passage of the chain. It should be de-
cidedly longer than the total length of the chain and when on the horse should project
past the mouthpiece and above it. It is not only a chain guard but it effectively pre-
vents the pinching between mouthpiece and chain described in Figure 45 page 69.

No. 9 shows the old military reversible bit. One side plain and smooth and the other
slightly corrugated. Even these slight corrugations were dropped before World War
One. Note the chain is a fixture and very long.

The links became progressively larger and thicker from each end of the chain until the centre links, which take the maximum pressure, were about twice the size of those at each end. This, too, increases the area of pressure.

Of course, to keep the enlarged links correctly centred, the length of the chain had to be adjusted each end for correct fitting and a curb hook each side became essential for such chains. This is now a standard practice. Although this was a slight improvement on the original chain, it still left much to be desired.

No chain previously produced is to be compared with the double-linked curb chain of today, either for efficiency or neatness. (See Nos. 3 to 8 above.) This chain has stood the test of more than half a century now and unless the new materials — plastics, nylon, fibre glass, etc., introduce something quite new, it looks like remaining standard usage. The old single-linked types are still available, however, and can be produced and sold more cheaply than the improved version. Some famous establishments still use them exclusively.

Protected Curb Chains

In high class riding where the horse is taught to relax and yield to the bit and also when the horse is habitually ridden on a loose rein, there is nothing to be gained by padding the curb chain. But with a pelham, and where a horse "takes hold" on a curb rein and the chain remains tight for some time, it is a definite advantage. A leather or felt pad is easily fitted.

Although in good hands a curb guard or pad is not necessary, I know of no circumstance where they are a disadvantage. In many cases they are a real benefit.

Adjusting the Curb Hook

Before using any particular curb bit for the first time, it is advisable to check that the curb hooks are set at a suitable gap. If the gap in the hook is too narrow, the chain has to be *forced* through the space each time it is put on. This results in a nasty jerk on the mouth for the horse when it is fitted on and also when it is removed.

The gap should be set so that you just "feel" the sides of the hook as the fitting link is slipped into position. The hooks are usually made of comparatively soft metal and it takes only a few seconds to prize them open a little with a screwdriver or to tap the edges a little closer if too wide. The adjustment has to be made only once.

If in doubt as to how tight the gap in the hook should be set, it is much to be preferred to have it a little too open than too close. The links should not have to be forced on and off, with the consequent jerk on the mouth it entails.

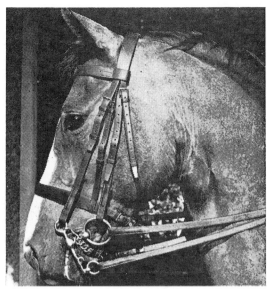

Figure 57.
The curb hooks that appear to
be up-side-down are carefully
made that way.
Notice how the bridoon keeps
the corners of the lips away
from the curb chain (See
Chapter 10) and prevents
pinching. This is a positive
advantage a double bridle has
over a pelham unless the
latter is specially designed.
The mouthpiece is very thick,
⅞" It seems not to
inconvenience the horse
although it is the first time
he has used it. Now we know
that the cannons of the bit do
not touch the bars of the
mouth there seems to be good
reason for making this part
of a port bit smaller.

The hooks on each side of the mouth should be given a decided cant or twist outwards, away from the lips, and should not be interchangeable from one side to the other as they almost invariably are today. The curb *hook* is not receiving the attention it deserves from either horseman or bit manufacturer. There is at least one firm of bit makers that puts the hook on in a manner that most of us would describe as "upside down." It is not a mistake but an improvement (see Figure 57). With the "normal" curb hook, almost everyone who has not been taught to do otherwise will place the links on the hook thumb nail up; with the type I have just mentioned the twist outwards extends to some 160° and results in almost everyone putting the link on with the nail turned downward. A good bit includes a good curb hook.

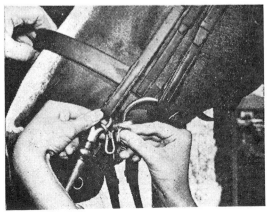

Figure 58.
Miss June Curtain, daughter
of our photographer. Placing
the chain on the hook
correctly. The chain is first
turned, clockwise, to its
fullest extent. It then becomes
flat and smooth. Then holding
the fitting link in the thumb
and forefinger as shown,
place the link on the
hook with the thumb nail
turned down. In this figure,
it is the second link
that is being hooked up.

85

Fitting the Curb Bit and Curb Chain

The curb bit should be fitted for height in the mouth *before* the curb chain is fitted for length

The exact position of the mouthpiece in the mouth has nowhere near the importance of the position of the curb chain at the back of the jaw.

Whatever the placing or height of the mouthpiece, *there is only one place for the curb chain and that is the chin groove,* where the bone under the skin is flat and smooth. The fitting of the Bit should ensure this. If the Bit is placed too high the chain will rest on the bumpy area where the two branches of the jaw meet; if higher still, the chain will rest on the sharp edges of the branches of the jaw itself. In either case it will worry the horse unduly.

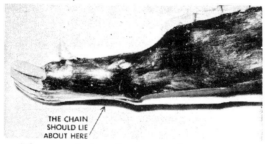

THE CHAIN
SHOULD LIE
ABOUT HERE

Figure 59.

A view of the bottom jaw showing normal protuberances just above the spot where the branches of the jaw meet. The smooth rounded surface just below the branches, is the chin-groove and is the most desirable spot for the curb chain to rest. The bumpy uneven surface higher up should be avoided as being much too painful.

The mouthpiece is not much affected if the Bit is a little too high or a little too low—but if the chain does not rest in the chin groove it can distract the horse's attention by being too painful.

The curb chain should be painless. It should be what is *in* the mouth that "speaks" to the horse. A painful curb chain distracts the animal's attention from the light signals he should be getting through the mouthpiece.

Curb chains range in size, and for preference buy one that when fitted will permit of an adjustment each way. When dropping links, of the six single links on the chain (three each side), drop the first link on the near side, and if still too long then drop the second and third links on the off-side. After that, the fourth on the near side. The objective is to hook up on the off-side so that either shortening or lengthening on the near side *remains possible.* Where two or three links are dropped on the one side, it is recommended that the end link be placed on the hook as shown in Figure 60 in order to stop the jingling.

How Long or Tight Should the Curb Chain Be?

No matter what the proportions of a Bit might be, its effectiveness will be considerably modified by the rein operating at a disadvantageous angle, i.e. any angle not a right-angle.

The curb bit is a lever and as with all levers, maximum effectiveness is obtained only when the operating force (the rein) acts at a right-angle to the lever (the cheek of the Bit).

86

Figure 60.
The 9th Lancer Bit. (Note this is a Bit, not a pelham).
This particular Bit is a very old one and has done a great deal of work. As was the practice of the time the single linked chain was a fixture to the off side and so all adjustments had to be made on the near side— Hence we see no less than 5 links "dropped" on the near side. In such a case the end link should be linked up first as described under "Old Military Instructions." When removing the bridle it is only necessary to remove the "fitting" link. (For hooking up the chain on a more modern Bit see the picture of Miss Ferrier's "Warwick" Frontispiece, Plate A). The Bit, already over 50 years old and now chrome plated, might well be in use for another 100 years for it has no moving parts to wear; but be sure you read what is said in Chapter 10 about loose curb chains before you use a 9th Lancer.

The important fact to be recognised is that a very tight curb chain — the horseman's expression is "when the Bit stands up" — will not only worry the horse incessantly, but will actually lessen the effectiveness of the rider's hand by varying the 90° angle. A dead loss for all concerned.

On the average horse the curb chain will be of a correct length when it permits the cheeks of the Bit to be drawn back and the chain to become just tight when the LINE OF THE CHEEKS OF THE BIT AND THE LINE OF THE HORSES LIPS FORM AN ANGLE OF 45°.

The angle of about 45° will be found most suitable for the average horse and it is favoured by almost all horsemen. With the cheeks of the Bit and the horse's lips making this angle, the other important angle — the Bit and the rein — will usually be found to approach the most effective — 90° — and only occasionally will the angle and height at which the head is carried affect it. With the occasional horse the 45° can be slightly varied, but it is seldom necessary to do so to any appreciable extent.

(Please note the use of the word "about" in relation to the angles; the degree of tension of the reins will cause it to be a little more or a little less from time to time.)

An angle of about 45° for cheek-bar to line of lips almost invariably produces the desired 90° angle of rein to cheek-bar.

A rough guide. When the chain is adjusted at the correct length it will be found that two fingers, placed sideways so that they are at a right angle to the chain, can be inserted between the chain and the jaw. This method of checking the length of the curb chain is often advocated. However, it is not recommended here except as a rough guide only, as it is effective only if the rider is careful to see that the cheeks of the Bit remain parallel with the line of the horse's lips. If the lower ends of the cheeks are allowed to move forward while making this test, two fingers can be admitted even when the chain is much too tight. Another reason for not recommending this method of adjustment is that most people do not realise that the "two fingers" must be at a *right-angle* to the chain, not parallel with it.

Figure 61.
A rough guide to the fitting of the correct length of chain is that it should admit two fingers, placed sideways and at a right angle to the chain, between it and the chin-groove, when the cheek-bar and the line of the horse's lips are parallel.
With the "up-side-down" type of hook shown the fitting link can be placed on the hook, with the thumb nail up and the hook itself will give the chain the final half turn downwards as it reaches the bottom. Good, clever.

This rough guide to the fitting of the curb chain is quite good and sufficient for most riders, but not for those who like to know their subject and to understand the "why" of everything.

Fitting of Curb Chain on Double Bridle

When the curb chain is fitted to a Bit forming part of a double bridle, the chain is always passed below the bridoon before being hooked up on the near side. If the chain is brought around above the bridoon the latter will prevent the chain resting in its proper place, the chin groove. Not only will it cause the chain to ride too high on the branches of the jaw, but each time the bridoon is in action it will oppose the curb chain, which will be resting above and against it. Both the Bit and bridoon will interfere with each other instead of co-operating harmoniously.

Remember that the bridoon should be slightly higher in the mouth than the Bit. Both the mouthpiece and the chain of the Bit should be lower than the bridoon and the chain should lie in the chin groove.

To Sum Up

The curb begins with the curb hooks. Put them in order before putting the Bit on the bridle.

See that the curb chain lies in the chin groove. It does least harm there.

The curb bit is most efficient when the operating rein makes an angle of 90° with the cheek bar of the bit. With the vast majority of horses this angle will exist when the cheek bar makes an angle of about 45° with the line of the horse's lips when the curb chain is in action. There are several distinct disadvantages if the chain is of such a length as to produce an angle of much more or much less than the recommended 45°.

A painful or irritating curb chain distracts the horse's attention from the mouthpiece — to which we want to direct his attention. Every effort has been made by the manufacturers to produce a painless curb chain. It is important that we use every endeavour to keep it painless.

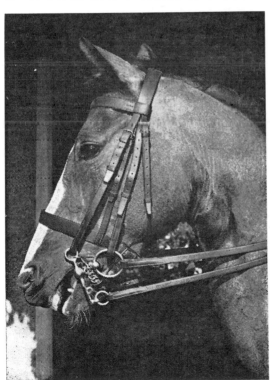

Figure 62

When the curb chain is the correct length the cheek-bar will make an angle of about 45° with the line of the horse's lips and the rein will operate at the most advantageous angle of 90° with the line of the cheek bar. When the Bit is fitted at the correct height in the mouth the curb chain will lie in the chin groove—where it causes the horse the least discomfort.

Small distractions become nagging irritations if maintained for long periods. A young horse takes little notice of these at first, but can become quite desperate about them if the irritations are continued for long.

Old Military Instructions (on the fitting of the curb chain).

Before leaving the subject of curb chains, let me draw your attention to the slight difference in the above directions from the old military instructions that used to be the guide for both cavalry and civilians. These instructions read:

"Grasp the end link of the chain (as described above) and first place the end link on the hook with the thumbnail turned up; then slide the hand back to the fitting link and place that link on the hook with the thumbnail turned downward."

Note the *fitting* link still "turned downward."

These directions still hold good for the single and equal-sized links as shown in Figures 56 page 83 and 60 page 87, as this type of chain does not need to be centred as the other two do and so all adjustments can be made from the near side. It is because it did not need to be centred that the single-linked chain with equal-sized links was favoured by our fighting services. The chain was, moreover, permanently fitted to the off-side so that it would not be lost or misplaced in the unpredictable circumstances of active service, and all adjustments had to be made to the near side, see Figure 60.

The chain also had to be left long enough to fit any horse in a Troop, and it was not at all unusual to have six to eight links spare and unwanted when the chain was fitted on a small-jawed horse. The end link had therefore to be hooked up first in order to dispose of some of this excess length. It also allowed the curb to be loosened only and not removed from the hook when taking the Bit out — important for quick re-saddling. All these conditions were important to the military man only, and do not need consideration today.

"But WHY the thumbnail up for the end link and nail downward for the fitting link?" might well be asked.

It doesn't matter, really, *as long as the fitting link is put on thumbnail downward* for the reason given previously — but you will find some difficulty in putting both links on the hooks with the nail downward: try it!

CHAPTER 13

RECOMMENDED PELHAMS AND BITS

*Smith & Brehens Pelham: The Scamperdale Pelham: The 9th Lancer Bit:
The Mullen-mouthed Pelham: The Three-in-one Pelham:
The Military Pelham: American Cowboy Bits:
The Jointed or Broken-mouthed Pelham: To Sum Up*

SMITH & BREHENS PELHAM

This little pelham is among the best general-service bits on the market today.

If you like a snaffle then use the top rein only, and you have a "Half-bar Snaffle" of good design. Moreover, if it has a jointed mouthpiece the centre will not drop in the mouth as does the ordinary snaffle. The chain, if you leave it on, and the lower cheek-bar, will check the bit being pulled through the horse's mouth, and the shape of the upper cheek ensures it does not interfere with the back teeth. Compare Figure 63 with a Half-bar Snaffle shown in Figure 65.

Used as a curb bit only it is almost identical with the 9th Lancer (see Figure 66), with the additional advantage that the chain cannot be made to pinch the lips no matter how it is fitted. The displacement of the hook to the rear ensures this. The illustrations show the similarity of the Half-moon Smith & Brehens (Figure 64) and the 9th Lancer (Figure 66).

Used as a Pelham it is a sort of improved snaffle, and I strongly recommend it FOR TRIAL with any horse not going well on a snaffle. It is a first-class bit for children, polo, polocross, novelty events in gymkhanas, and jumping. I noticed several riders using it at the Marrabel Rodeo, 1966,

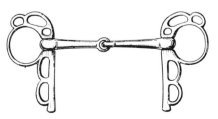

*Figure 63.
A Smith and Brehens broken or jointed Pelham with the curb hooks removed.*

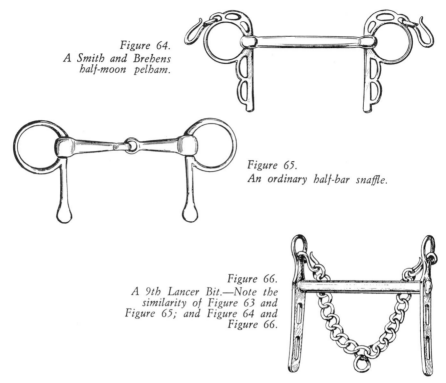

Figure 64.
A Smith and Brehens
half-moon pelham.

Figure 65.
An ordinary half-bar snaffle.

Figure 66.
A 9th Lancer Bit.—Note the
similarity of Figure 63 and
Figure 65; and Figure 64 and
Figure 66.

and in the Adelaide Royal Show the same year three of the harness horses used it!

Thousands are in use already because the bit has been found to be satisfactory when tried. It is not recommended, however, for the type of puller that leans on the bit and gets the rider to "carry its head for it."

I noticed, too, at the Marrabel Rodeo that the riders used a length of leather thong in place of a curb chain. The thong was crossed from curb hook to curb hook several times before knotting at the side. It is not unfastened when the bridle is removed.

Like the 9th Lancer which it resembles in so many respects, the Smith & Brehens will not catch up on a wire fence. It looks a "fancy" sort of bit to men of the old school, who like bits to be plain, but there is not one unnecessary feature in it.

The Smith & Brehens is available with a jointed or half-moon mouthpiece, but the mouthpiece is often made too thin in the jointed variety and unfortunately I have not seen it in other than soft metal. In any case, I prefer the half-moon.

If I were asked to suggest a bit as a "Pony Club Bit" I would suggest the Smith & Brehens, or one designed on the same lines, as an alternative to a snaffle.

THE SCAMPERDALE PELHAM

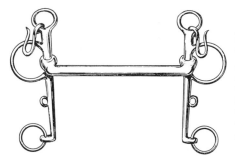

Figure 67.
The "Scamperdale Pelham.
The 90° bend at each end of
the mouthpiece sets the cheek-
bars back so that even with a
very loose curb chain the lip
cannot become trapped
between the mouthpiece and
the chain. A recommended
pelham.

A well-designed bit that cannot pinch the lips. Strongly recommended for polo and similar pursuits, it should be seen much more often than it is. A very good bit.

It can be strongly recommended for all sports. It is of good proportions; its thick straight mouthpiece is very mild in action, and the mouthpiece is taken forward in a manner that effectively prevents pinching of the lips by the curb chain. Its only defect is that the bottom ring can get trapped in a wire fence.

THE 9th LANCER BIT

I have already made mention of the usefulness of this excellent and mild Bit, with its plain neat appearance. See Figure 66 and Figure 45 page 69.

Wherever I see one being used on a polo pony, this Bit seems to give satisfaction to both pony and rider. Its mild lever action softly locks the Bit on to the jaw and so the mouthpiece is restrained from working up and around the molar teeth.

It is a very good Bit, although no better than the Smith & Brehens Pelham just described—which is more or less an improved 9th Lancer. The Smith & Brehens cannot pinch the skin at the lips if the curb chain is fitted too long, whereas the 9th Lancer can. Neither of them lend themselves to being caught up in a wire fence.

I like, and recommend, the half-moon or port mouthpiece of about $\frac{5}{8}''$ thickness.

Remember, horses go better on this Bit (as on most Bits) if ridden with a loose rein rather than a loose curb chain. Use the leather rings shown in Figure 10 page 25 or the long curb guard shown in Figure 45 page 69.

93

THE MULLEN-MOUTHED PELHAM

Figure 68.
The "Mullen mouthed
Pelham." A recommended
bit but it can pinch the lip—
as can be seen in this
photograph—if the precautions
recommended in Chapter 10
are not taken.

This is a half-moon shaped mouthpiece covered with hard rubber, usually almost an inch thick. I have already spoken favourably of the mouthpiece in Chapter 7. The half-moon shape is a good one and the hard rubber makes it easy on the horse's mouth without being easy enough to invite him to take liberties with it

Do not confuse this mouthpiece with the soft flexible rubber one which suits only an occasional mouth.

The GREAT FAULT with this bit and many other pelhams is that the chain can cause very serious pinching—so do not use it without taking one of the precautions set out in Chapter 10. With the lips properly protected against pinching, the Mullen Mouthed Pelham will be found to be an excellent bit for several types of difficult mouths—and a very good bit the polo and similar pursuits. Figure 68 above shows how the lip can be pinched by the chain against the mouthpiece (see also Figure 46 page 70).

THE THREE-IN-ONE PELHAM

This little bit is of quite unusual design, different in many respects from almost any other bit on the market. The cheeks are capable of revolving the full 360°; there is no downward pull on the poll as there is with most curb bits; the mouthpiece is thick (which thoughtless people think makes for severity); it will not reach as far up as the first molar; and, most important of all, there is the corkscrew-like curb hook.

The unusual features of this bit are all good ones and aim to make the bit almost fool-proof. The maker had still to induce riders believing that only brute force and pain would stop a horse, to avoid the use of force. This he did by frightening them—by telling them that his "severe" bit was capable of breaking the horse's jaw! This worked very well.

The bit is, in fact, a particularly mild one. Every feature of it has been very carefully thought out, aiming either to serve a special purpose or to

Figure 69.
The "Three-in-One" Pelham.
A lip strap should always be used with this pelham as the bit can revolve about the mouthpiece a full 360° without it, when the horse tosses his head. The loose rings act as "spacers" and so prevent pinching of the lip between curb chain and mouthpiece.
Shown is Miss D. Spurling's "Arrawidgee Lass." A very excitable and energetic little mare, she is at her best and calmest when ridden lightly in this port-mouthed Pelham. Recommended.

avoid a fault other bits might have. The queer curb-hook, for instance, you may think only fanciful. But if you are observant, you will find that:

(1) it isn't possible to adjust the curb-chain too tightly—you need a certain amount of slack in the chain to get it on the hook at all;

(2) the twist in the hook automatically gives the chain that last half-turn so important for the correctly fitted curb chain;

(3) the pinching of the lip between the cheek bar and curb chain cannot occur with this hook, even if the chain is fitted too loosely.

If you are looking for a severe bit try the Three-in-One—but do remember "This bit is capable of breaking a horse's jaw if used with severity."

Even the name, "Three-in-One" is impressive to all who don't realise that every pelham is three bits in one: Snaffle, Bit and Pelham.

A good bit.

The Three-in-One, however, has a fault common to many curb bits used in Europe—the bottom rein ring will catch up in a wire fence and so also will the curb hooks. A serious fault and in the outback an insuperable objection, as it is no joke to have a broken bridle and a loose horse in a paddock measured by square miles.

95

THE MILITARY PELHAM

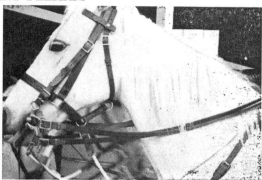

Figure 70. The "Universal" Pelham. Standard bit and bridle for all British Mounted forces. Used also by the South Australian Police for "active" duty.
Note that the noseband is not used as an ornament but is a serviceable halter when the bit headstall is released at the top to allow the bit to be removed and replaced quickly, in the manner we recommend for drop nosebands. The bottom rein is in the "normal" position. Troops are forbidden to use the bottom "D" but the steady progress toward milder bits has not yet reached the stage where the bottom "D" is abandoned. Recommended. This pelham will neither pinch the lips nor pull through the mouth easily.

This is another good bit although not particularly attractive in appearance. It suits almost every type of mouth and it was listed in military stores as "Universal, reversible port-mouthed bit." It could be used to advantage on any and all horses. When first introduced early in the century, it was corrugated one side, but soon after was available only with a wholly smooth mouthpiece. The days of severe bits were over.

The off-set lower cheek prevents pinching by the curb chain, stops the bit pulling through the mouth, and makes it difficult for a horse to take the cheek or rein in his teeth. When used with two reins, as it is intended to be used, the two topmost positions are recommended.

The Military Pelham was essentially a military bit and will almost certainly disappear in the course of time, although it deserves to live on. My main purpose in showing it is that it illustrates the effect of setting back the lower cheek to prevent pinching by the curb chain.

The size of each bit was permanently stamped into the metal—"L," "M" and "S." A good practice.

AMERICAN COWBOY BITS

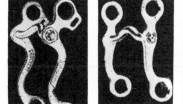

Figure 71. Some Bits of the type I call "Cowboy Bits."

I have called them that because in this country we seldom see them except in western cowboy films! Most of our riders condemn them as being severe yet it is exceptional to see them used with the rein even momentarily tight.

True the cheeks are long; but the horses are trained to go on a loose rein and when well ridden the trained horse responds long before the rein becomes tight. The long cheek permits the rein to be moved quite a distance before the curb becomes tight and long before that happens the horse feels the movement and has an opportunity to stop before the bit becomes painful. A bit of such proportions *could* be made severe, but as we have pointed out so often if the horse has warning of a coming demand, he will anticipate it. He has a chance to say "What am I waiting for?" and so can avoid the pain that a quick pull on a snaffle always causes.

I don't propose to say much about this type of Bit for they are "not quite our smoking." As with all bits, so much depends upon how they are used.

They have several desirable features: they are designed not to catch up on a wire fence; they usually have the lower cheek back-swept so that pinching by the curb cannot occur; and a strap is frequently substituted for a curb chain.

You may have noticed that a foot of light chain is often fitted to the curb rein ring and that the end of the rein is buckled to the chain. This means that the light chain has to be lifted before the rein becomes tight, thus giving the horse even more, and gentler, warning of the rider's coming demand.

Let us keep an open mind on these Bits—I have a feeling we have something to learn about the handling of them and the preparation of the horse for them.

They are suited only to loose rein riding, remember. More about these Bits in Chapter 10 and see Figure 43 page 67.

THE JOINTED OR BROKEN-MOUTHED PELHAM
See Figure 15 page 27.

Using the curb rein of a Bit or Pelham with a jointed mouthpiece can be compared to using a block of wood as a fulcrum in mud. In an instance where there is a weight to be lifted, the block of wood disappears into the mud as soon as it is subjected to sufficient pressure, instead of lifting the weight. So it is with any jointed mouthpiece or flexible rubber mouthpiece used with a curb. The mouthpiece, which represents the fulcrum, is not stable enough to be effective to the usual extent.

When a jointed mouthpiece is used with a curb chain it is invariably in the form of a pelham. There is a good deal to be said for a jointed mouthpiece as a pelham, but little or nothing to be said in its favour as a Bit.

Although ineffective for the normal purpose of a curb, the jointed pelham serves a purpose and has a usefulness not often recognised. For in-

97

stance, quite a number of beginners use a jointed pelham and find it most satisfactory. "Mind over matter" may be said in explanation, "the riders think the curb gives them extra power—which gives them confidence—and that is all they really need."

There is some truth in that contention too, although it is not the full story. Certainly it is a fact that many young riders do get on well with this type of bit, and seem to hold and control their ponies easier with it even though the curb is almost ineffective. Its main virtue is that it can clamp lightly on the jaw without locking rigidly to it. There is a good deal of springiness and give about it that absorbs many of the shocks of a roughish hand.

With children and beginners generally, this roughness is usually unintentional and unnoticed by the rider. The jointed pelham absorbs or reduces the severity of the roughness.

To Sum Up

A well-proportioned jointed pelham has its uses. For everyday riding, it has most of the good qualities of a snaffle and few of the faults of other types of curbs. The rider who likes to be "right," the dressage rider and the show rider, generally "won't have a bar of it;" but, for the reasons given, quite a number of riders do well with it. It suits certain hands rather than certain mouths.

If you are buying one, make sure you select one with a mouthpiece not less than ½″ thick. For some reason they are usually made very thin. The curb chain with a broken pelham can be adjusted rather shorter than is recommended with an ordinary Bit, as it won't get really tight anyway.

A pelham can become a snaffle. See Chapter 17 "Getting the Tongue over the Bit" on this subject.

CHAPTER 14

MARTINGALES AND NOSEBANDS

Irish Martingales: Running Martingales:
Standing Martingales or "Standards": Fitting the noseband:
How long should the martingale be: The Martingale and the Hackamore:

The Irish Martingale

This is a simple strap about 6" in length with a ring sewn at each end. It is worn or used under the neck just behind the snaffle, a rein being passed through each ring.

Young horses and horses with the habit of tossing their heads, sometimes get the two reins on one side of the neck. The Irish Martingale prevents this. It is most commonly seen on gallopers, and we need say no more about it here except that it also to some extent stops the snaffle pulling through the horse's mouth in a tussle.

The Running Martingale

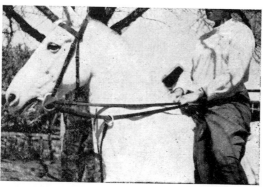

Figure 72. Miss C. Roberts with "Alpine Prince" showing a Running Martingale with large bone rings as recommended. The Martingale is also of a recommended length; long enough to reach about the height of the wither. Notice, too, the "stops" on the reins to prevent the martingale rings becoming caught on the rein buckle.
Note, too, the sheep skin under the weight bearing parts of the saddle only, so as not to add extra width to the horse under the rider and where neither horse or rider needs the padding.

This consists of an adjustable strap running from the centre of the girth between the horse's forelegs, to the reins. The upper end of the strap is split down the centre and the reins run through rings sewn or buckled to the ends of these straps.

By passing the backstay of the noseband through the two rings, a running martingale can also be used as a standing martingale.

Reins passed through the rings of a running martingale should, for preference, be sewn, not buckled to the snaffle ring. If an ordinary buckled rein is used, it should have a leather "stop" fitted to prevent the ring of the martingale slipping over the rein-buckle. This sometimes happens and if precautions have not been taken, it can produce disastrous effects. The sudden jerk given the horse's head when he raises it will cause some horses to throw themselves back, sometimes on to the rider.

Use thick rings. If rubber-covered, laced or other variations of non-slip reins are used, avoid the small and sometimes thin brass rings usually fitted to martingales today. Larger and thicker bone rings are obtainable and should be used on such reins. In all cases, the reins should slide or run easily through the rings, and the thicker variety of ring is best in any event. There is also no need for the rubber covering or the lacing to be taken too far along the reins.

The Standing Martingale or "Standard"

Figure 73.
Miss C. Whyntie showing a Standing Martingale of a recommended length. The horse has only been dressed for demonstration purposes as it is a three-year-old and so will be "teething" for at least the next 12 months or more. Nosebands, standing martingales and full-bar snaffles are not recommended for horses under 5 years. Full explanations in Chapter 4.

The standing martingale is similar to the running martingale except that it is adapted for fastening to the noseband. Sometimes it is split down from the upper end like the running variety, so that its two ends can, if desired, be buckled to the snaffle ring. This is a practice we cannot recommend, however. If you have become so desperate, you would do better to consider the use of Market Harborough, described in Chapter 15 — next following.

You can definitely strap the horse's head down with a "standard." Unless it is fitted reasonably long, as is recommended, the horse fights it—keeps it tight the whole time he is moving. If it is put on too tightly at first, many horses will throw themselves backward on to the rider when they first feel their heads strapped down—this being another instance of a horse naturally and by instinct resisting force. Even if you intend to use a short martingale, you will be well advised to start off with it long and only shorten it progressively.

A standing martingale is used on a great number of polo ponies. It positively limits the height to which the horse can lift his head. In Chapter 7 we have looked into the reasons for an excessively high head carriage and the poking out of the nose that goes with it. Special bits are recommended, but in any case most polo ponies go better in a standard than without it.

However, *some horses behave very badly in a standing martingale.* When a standing martingale is tight, as it usually is most of the time a horse is moving, in addition to the pressure on the face there is very great pressure on the cheeks at the SIDE of the head where the noseband is drawn tight as it passes over the molars of the upper jaw. In Chapter 4 the horse's head has been described and attention drawn to the fact that the upper molars are at the widest part of the animal's head. See Figure 7 page 17. The heavy and constant pressure of the noseband will be right over the sharp edges of these teeth.

Young horses still in the teething process can be driven to desperation by the constant pressure and agonising pain, and they will soon be behaving very badly. Of course, the pony could avoid the pain by keeping the head down and the martingale loose, but again I stress "horses are not made that way. They resist and fight great pain." It is impossible to get good work from a horse in these circumstances, and unless you do something to correct the situation, serious trouble lies ahead.

If the animal is less than five years old, remove not only the martingale but the noseband as well—at least until the horse has all his teeth through. With an older horse, filing his teeth may make all the difference, or even moving the noseband up or down with the idea of getting away from any possible sore spot. If you use a standing martingale, a regular veterinary check of the teeth would be a sound investment.

Pack the Noseband. It is possible to pack or pad the inside of the noseband at the front to keep the sides out clear of the cheeks—something similar to what is called a "blind" in trotting circles. Each noseband should be individually fitted in such a case. Do not use padding at the SIDES OVER the teeth, as this will increase the pressure on the very spot where it should be avoided.

I have never heard of anyone using a Standard buckled to the rings of a drop noseband, and I hesitate to say "Try it." But if your pony is behaving badly and you feel you must continue to use a standing martingale, I am sure he would be grateful if you tried it. Certainly it would be better than buckling to the bit.

FITTING THE NOSEBAND

Never use a drop noseband just above the bit. And never put anything tight on the head just above the bit. The bit—a snaffle particularly—moves up the jaw and if it approaches a tight noseband, the lips can become badly pinched. Even an ordinary noseband, especially if fitted very low, can become very tight if the horse opens his mouth wide as some young horses do.

I dislike the ordinary noseband (not a "Cavesson" as it is sometimes called—a cavesson is a special headstall made for lunging, disciplining, and training a horse, and usually has a steel reinforcement among other things). The ordinary noseband has served no useful purpose since the days of the military horse where it was used as a tie-up halter when on service. But if you do use one, never tolerate one that has the headstall looped around the noseband. The headstall should be stitched on the *outside* of the noseband, and even the stitches should be boned smooth on the inside. ALLOW NOTHING TO PROJECT INSIDE ANY STRAP THAT CAN BECOME TIGHT, PARTICULARLY IF THE STRAP LIES CLOSE TO A BONE. No-one should use a stand-

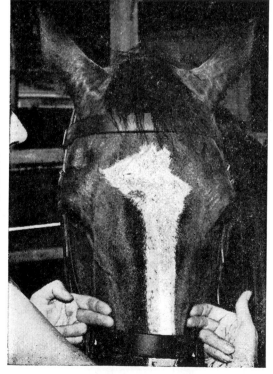

Figure 74.
The noseband should be fitted for height first and should lie not less than 2 fingers below the projecting cheek bones.

ing martingale on an ordinary noseband who is not familiar with all the facts set out in Chapter 4. Beware of all the possible repercussions when you use a standing martingale.

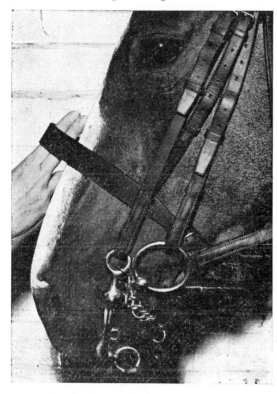

Figure 75.
Having been first fitted for height, the noseband should then be buckled to admit of not less than two fingers— (at a right angle to the noseband)—between it and the face.

One thing—a wide noseband used on a horse with a very big head has the effect of making that head seem smaller!

HOW LONG SHOULD THE MARTINGALE BE?

A horse's head is generally considered to be not too high until it is raised above the level of the withers, and generally the martingale should be of such a length as not to interfere with the horse's head until it is raised above that level.

Our aim should be, not to try to pull the head down, but to induce or encourage the horse to relax and drop it down himself to a natural level— just relaxing will do it.

Correctly fitted, the martingale, standing or running, should reach almost to the height of the withers as shown in Figures 72 and 73 pages 99 and 100. If much shorter than this, it still remains in action after the horse has brought his head down to the correct level. We should never lose sight of the main principle of horse training—to encourage the horse when he does what we want and discourage him when he does other than that.

The running martingale is sometimes fitted shorter than I have just recommended. In some cases the rider is only interested, not in the height or angle of the head, but in preventing the bit pulling up the mouth towards the molar teeth. The shorter martingale gives a downward direction to the rein, tending to keep the snaffle on the bars of the mouth. In these cases it usually pays to use a second rein that acts in the normal way. A pelham is a better proposition.

There can be no doubt that a second rein with a running martingale can be an advantage at times when riding a very green young horse. It ensures keeping the bit on to the bars of the mouth to some extent, should he get out of hand. Here again it pays to use a second rein so that you can use the martingale or not, as you find most advantageous.

Friction Plays an Important Part with a running martingale, running reins, and Market Harboroughs. This means that the passive end of the reins never receives the full effect from the active end. With a horse that thrusts his head out, a good deal of the force is absorbed by the martingale, and conversely, a good deal of the effect of a rough hand does not reach the horse's mouth. We should always be fully conscious of this. It can be very important, both in causing trouble and dealing with it. Running reins and Market Harboroughs are considered in Chapter 15—next following.

Very few show judges will consider a horse that wears a martingale in the ring, as it advertises the fact that the horse has a difficulty that the rider has been unable to correct in the usual manner.

Figure 76.
A Hackamore.

THE HACKAMORE

I have never used a hackamore but I would expect it to be equal to the best of the bits if properly handled.

Like the American Cowboy Bits, the hackamore is no good for a horse or rider that "hangs on," but should be used on a loose rein. One type of hackamore can be seen in Figure 76.

Our photo shows a stock horse that did an excellent job at Marrabel Rodeo in 1966 although she was very "edgy" and timorous. She was ridden on the Hackamore shown above and I made a point of looking to see what made her so touchy, as hackamores, well used as this one was, are not usually upsetting.

THE NOSEBAND proved to be the trouble. It was made of some plaited material and drawn together at the back where the STANDING MARTINGALE was attached. A raw spot caused by the chafing of the plaited material is clearly visible on the back of the lower jaw some 2 inches above the present line of the noseband.

If a standing martingale IS used it is imperative that the noseband is *smooth*. It makes for the horse's comfort if the backstay is spread somewhat, not drawn together to chafe the jaw.

Neither browband or throatlash is needed with this type of headstall having a "split Head."

CHAPTER 15

REINS — AND RUNNING REINS

Correct way to hold: Light reins: Laced, string or rubber-covered reins:
The polo rein: Reins of a double bridle: Buckle joining ends of reins:
Running reins: How the running rein works: The Market Harborough

How to Hold the Reins

I don't propose to tell you how to hold them, for in my opinion there is no such thing as "the" correct way to hold them. It is the old story again, "what is best is right," so what is right will vary with what we are doing at the time.

Good horsemen are no more hidebound about the way in which the reins are held than they are about other matters that are not constant. Most change their hold on the reins with different horses and in different circumstances, but almost all agree that whether you hold the reins in one hand or two, cross them or keep them parallel, use a bridge or keep them separate, have one finger between them or several, or none—however you arrange them, hold them as lightly in the fingers as the situation permits.

HOLD THE REINS IN THE FINGERS, NOT IN THE FIST. Have them normally, well down the fingers and the fingers partly open—not at the base of the fingers and gripped in the full of the hand. When you need to hold them more firmly THEN close the fingers, tight if necessary, and without hesitation; but the moment the horse behaves, then again partly open the fingers and be agreeable—so that he can reap the reward of being "a good boy."

Remember, the horse behaves in order to obtain relief from whatever we are doing at the moment. It is the *discontinuance* of the pain or inconvenience that produces results. If you are not light, he cannot be.

Light Reins

Light thin reins, or "ribbons," have always been recommended as tending to produce light hands and light mouths. Thick wide reins tend to produce heavier hands unless the rider takes care to hold them lightly in the fingers whenever the circumstances permit.

If you hold the reins like an axe, you'll tend to use them like an axe.

Laced, String or Rubber-covered Reins

Reins wet with rain or sweat tend to slip through the fingers and are hard to hold, putting the rider at a disadvantage. Laced, rubber-covered and string reins stop the slipping. Use them when you feel it necessary, but they do tend to make you heavier with your hands. I prefer an ordinary rein with a bight taken around the fingers as shown in Figures 77, 78 and 79. It both shortens the reins instantly and also makes it easy to hold them with partly opened fingers, and you can drop the bight again—instantly.

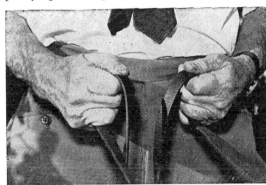

Figure 77.
When the horse is pulling hard, and wet reins tend to slip although we hold them until the fingers tire, try making a bight around the fingers as shown in lower figures.

Figure 78.
It takes only part of a second to extend the forefinger and place it under the rein—in this manner and ...

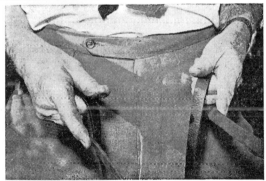

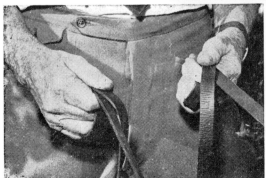

Figure 79.
... bring it and the rein back to the thumb again. This shortens the rein several inches and stops the slipping and allows the fingers a litle rest.
The bight can be released and the rein lengthened again just as quickly and easily. Don't maintain the shortened rein a moment longer than is necessary.

The Polo Rein

The polo rein is much shorter than an ordinary rein and has a special fitting (or one on each side) which allows it to be shortened or lengthened.

The rein is adjustable for length so that it can be held in the full of the left hand without the usual loop coming up between the thumb and forefinger. It cannot, of course, slip through the fingers. The exact length required varies with different riders and different ponies.

It is usually made wider than an ordinary rein, which is both a pity and a fault. The polo rein is very convenient when playing that or any similar game where a short rein is used throughout. It is most inconvenient for any other purpose and is usually exchanged for an ordinary rein when play is finished—riding or leading a pony home or for exercise, for instance.

Occasionally the polo rein is made with a non-slip rubber cover. Why, is incomprehensible, as the rein can't slip anyway. It merely adds to the cost and to the bulk of rein held in the hand.

A serious defect not often recognised is that the rider holds the reins in the full of the hand—in the fist—instead of between the fingers as is customary and best with a normal rein. Thus the thick non-slip rein, held in the closed fist instead of the fingers, is usually used with much more force and strength than is the same rider's custom with an ordinary rein—*and he seldom recognises that he is doing so.*

This is a most serious fault with a polo rein, as the excitement of the game tends to make us all unduly rough with our hands even when using a normal rein. The polo rein is a great convenience but unless the rider recognises the additional power it gives the hand, and uses it with discretion, it tends to be very severe on the pony's mouth. You cannot get good polo— or any other game for that matter—from a pony constantly on edge from fear of the bit.

An adjusting buckle of a polo rein can be seen in Figure 10 page 25.

Reins of a Double Bridle

Of the two reins of a double bridle, one, the top rein, is usually $\frac{5}{8}''$ wide and the other, the bottom, is usually about $\frac{1}{2}''$ wide. The top rein is intended to be wider than the other.

This is because the top rein goes to the bridoon, or snaffle, and is the main riding rein. A wide rein is held more firmly in the hand than a narrow one and so the working or duty rein is made wider; this ensures it being held a little firmer than the bottom or Bit rein, which is thinner.

The bottom rein of a double bridle is only intended to control the angle ¬: which the horse carries his head. If he pokes his nose out from the required angle, the still, quiet rein, *automatically* brings the curb into action. THE RIDER ADJUSTS ITS LENGTH; THE HORSE OPERATES IT.

There used to be one other difference between the reins of a double bridle—the top or main rein had a buckle in the centre and the light bottom rein did not—it was sewn in the centre. This is still the usual practice, but whereas the reins used to be sewn together as shown in Figure 80 below, they are now almost invariably sewn as in Figure 81. There were trifling advantages in the old methods; why, I wonder, have we abandoned them?

Fig. 80   Fig. 81

Figue 80 shows how the ends of the bit reins were joined in past days. It has one or two slight advantages over the modern method shown in the Figure 81 next.

Figure 82. A suitable join for the ends of the snaffle reins. The rein is reduced in size to a "waist" and a small buckle with a curved edge used to ensure the rein breaks at this point if a hitched horse "pulls back." The rein then still remains serviceable.

BUCKLE JOINING THE ENDS OF REINS

This might be a good place to mention the D-shaped half buckle which may be seen in several of the bridles used in the illustrations of this book. The D buckle has a curved front on the side away from where the tongue is fastened. Never buy a bridle that uses them, for a moment's consideration will convince you that they will break leather much more readily than those with a straight edge. See the one in Figure 82 above.

The D-shaped half buckle is the best to use for joining the ends of reins for the very reason that it WILL break the leather much easier; there, where it does least damage.

Australian Stockmen often use a long leather lace or thong to join the centre of the reins; not only can it be used time after time, as often as it is broken, but it can also be used for other repairs in an emergency.

RUNNING REINS

There are three types of Running Reins in use with which I am familiar. Some riders seem to find them useful, and it might be advisable to review these reins and the effects they produce. In each of them, the rein is passed THROUGH the snaffle rings instead of being buckled to them. The rein "runs" through the cheek rings.

(1)   One type runs from the rider's hands through the rings of the snaffle and then is taken upwards and either buckled to the end of a bit-headstall, or joined together over the head. The action of this type is very similar to that of a Gag Snaffle, although with a running rein the snaffle "runs" up and down much more readily. It tends to raise the head and bring the nose in—it is said.

(2)   A second type also runs from the rider's hands through the rings of the snaffle, but is then taken back towards the saddle. Its ends may be attached either to the saddle or to the girth. This aims to bring the nose in but without raising the head higher.

(3)   A third type resembles a martingale in some respects; it loops around the girth and is adjustable at that point for length. It is then passed upward between the forelegs and through a neckstrap. After that it is split into two straps, each of which is passed through a snaffle ring and *ultimately buckled to the ordinary snaffle rein.* The buckle is sewn to the snaffle rein some 12″ from the snaffle.

I have heard this type of running rein called a "Market Harborough." When properly fitted, it could have all the advantages of the other varieties without their disadvantages.

Not everyone approves of running reins. Although I have never used them I hesitate to condemn them, but we should understand how they operate.

How the Running Rein Works

All types of running reins act on the same principle as a block and tackle. One end of the tackle (the rein) is fixed and the other is then passed through the block (snaffle) which has previously been attached to the object to be affected (the horse's head). The loose or running end is then taken on to the power unit (our hands).

For every foot the hand draws the rein backwards, the bit will be moved only 6 inches. (Maximum.)

The rider can put double the weight on the bit with the same effort (and this is a danger), but he can *resist* much more easily the force of a horse when he thrusts his head out.

If a running rein is used by the rider to resist the horse's forward thrust *only,* it could be useful.

If it is used by the rider to increase his own tension on the reins it increases the severity of his hands at the bit, and this is a real danger. It becomes the proverbial "razor in the hands of a monkey."

If the rein is used like a martingale to control the angle and height of the head, although not to be compared with the skilful use of a snaffle and ordinary rein, it might on occasion be useful.

If used to control pace and direction, its use can be disastrous—and I don't use the word figuratively!

So, if used at all, the running rein, other than a Market Harborough, should be in conjunction with an ordinary snaffle and ordinary snaffle rein. It should be an additional rein, not a substitute.

Figure 83. The "Market Harborough" and a cross over "drop noseband." Mr. Robert Goldsworthy on his A Grade show jumper "Fifinella" which has been regularly jumped successfully on a well fitted Market Harborough and the noseband and soft rubber snaffle shown.
If the rider shortens the reins—i.e. brings the horse's nose in further—the running rein section of the rein "cuts out." If on the other hand the horse pokes his nose out from the position shown (where the running rein section is just stretched) the ordinary rein section "cuts out" and the other, with its pulley action, takes over.
Not recommended for general use. Too much depends upon the skill of the rider who must be able and ready to "throw the reins" to the horse when landing if the situation requires it. So much depends upon the rider's ability to "feel."

THE MARKET HARBOROUGH

The Market Harborough seems to combine the use of the running rein and the ordinary rein and to some extent the running martingale. When correctly adjusted, the running rein section is not operative until the horse's head is extended out too far.

There is a very real danger in all types of running reins on jumping horses. A horse must be able to extend his head as he crosses the highest point of his jump; a running rein in insensitive hands could quickly spoil a promising jumper.

I don't recommend them but they could have their uses. I'll need to watch them—try them—before I could recommend them. If you try one,

111

be light, be moderate, be sympathetic with your hands—particularly if jumping.

Everything depends upon how a Market Harborough is fitted and how it is used. When properly fitted, the running rein section comes into action only when the horse's nose goes out or up too far. It *should be operated by the horse* and it should automatically become inoperative as soon as the horse assumes a normal carriage.

In good hands they could be safe and useful.

In unskilled hands they could be dangerous. And don't flatter yourself —the horse will soon straighten you out if you are kidding yourself about your skill!

Correct adjustment is most important with this running rein.

CHAPTER 16

DROP NOSEBANDS

When should a drop noseband be used?: Purpose of drop noseband:
Correct construction: Fitting the drop noseband:
Nothing new in drop noseband: Variations:

Figure 84.
A correctly fitted drop-
noseband, although we
recommend sewing the buckle
to the shorter strap.

The use of improperly made and badly fitted drop nosebands is so common
and the discomfort caused the unfortunate horse is often so great, that I
welcome the opportunity to explain the "why" and "how" of the drop
noseband.

When Should a Drop Noseband be Used?

Generally, whenever there is any doubt as to the advisability of using some
gadget or other on a horse, the best advice is "don't use it." Use nothing
that is not needed and nothing that serves no useful purpose.

Nothing should be used on a riding horse merely for decoration or show.

Like so many other gadgets used with horses, drop nosebands have their
uses and serve their turn—and having done so should be discarded. A drop

noseband is not necessary on a trained horse, and, like a martingale, its use should be proof positive that the training is as yet imperfect or incomplete. Like a "Road under Repair" sign, the sign should be removed when the job is done!

Drop nosebands do, by force, literally prevent a horse opening his mouth too far, but they do not altogether prevent him pulling or setting his jaw. They can help—but the real job of educating the mouth still lies ahead of the rider.

Purpose of the Drop Noseband

The uses of the drop noseband are:
(1) to prevent or correct the habit of opening the mouth and to help induce the horse to yield at the poll instead of with the jaw only;
(2) to prevent rather than correct, the troublesome habit of getting the tongue over the bit;
(3) by keeping the mouth closed, check to some extent the tendency for the bit to pull through the sides of the horse's mouth in a struggle.

They are not necessary although you may find them useful in the early days of training. When properly fitted drop nosebands do no harm, but they should be discarded as soon as possible, and *always* before a double bridle is used.

Why not the Ordinary Noseband? The object of the drop noseband is to keep the horse's mouth closed; or to be more precise, to prevent him opening his mouth excessively. The lower the drop noseband is fitted, the easier it will keep the mouth closed, so it is placed as low as possible—actually below the snaffle. If we tried to use an ordinary noseband in this position the front of it would press on the soft flexible bones of the nostrils, and so interfere with the horse's breathing. The drop noseband has therefore been designed so that while the front stay will remain up above the nostrils, the BACK-STAY WILL DROP and lie in the chin groove, below the snaffle.

See that Your Drop Noseband is Correctly Made

It is most important, if the drop noseband is to operate successfully and without worrying the horse, that the saddler does not make the front-stay too long. It should be short enough to keep the rings at least 2″ in front of the line of the lips. If made shorter than this it will do no harm; but if longer, when the front stay is at the correct height, it will cause the back stay to foul the snaffle as it passes to the chin groove, either forcing the snaffle up or riding over the top of it—often doing one thing on one side of the mouth and the other on the opposite side.

Check, too, that the back stay is correctly made; the strap on the *near* side should not be longer than 3″ including the buckle, which should be at the end of *this strap*. Again, if it is shorter it does no harm; but if longer, the buckle will bite into the bone of the chin groove when the band is tight. A shorter strap keeps the buckle at the side of the mouth, where there is no bone to press on.

The buckle should be at the end of the SHORT strap which should be on the NEAR side.

KEEP THE HORSE COMFORTABLE

It has already been stressed in Chapter 2 that in the control and education of any horse it is most important that we keep the horse from any discomforts that may distract his attention from what we are doing. A throatlash that is too tight; a browband too short; a bit too high or too low in the mouth; an improperly made or ill-fitted noseband; a strap pressing on or near a sore or tender area—any one of these things (and many others too) can in a very short time become irksome and irritating, eventually completely upsetting even a quiet-tempered horse.

Such things start bad habits such as boring on the bit, tossing the head, pulling, jogging and not walking, or many other really troublesome habits which often persist long after the original cause has been removed.

A badly constructed drop noseband can be a real cause of discomfort and trouble.

Fitting the Drop Noseband

When properly made the drop noseband is simple to fit. Firstly *remove the ordinary noseband* if you have one on your snaffle bridle (you alone know why you have it on) and replace it with the drop noseband.

Put the bridle on and adjust the snaffle. A snaffle, unlike a Bit, should be fitted well up into the corners of the lips. Then adjust the drop noseband so that the front stay is above the soft flexible bones of the nostrils. Pass the longer strap of the back stay from the off side, under the snaffle, and buckle it up—at first fairly loosely. The horse should have become used to the feel of it after a few days and it should then be correctly adjusted, just tight enough to allow the comfortable insertion of ONE finger between the back stay and the chin groove.

The front stay should be above the nostrils, the rings should be not less than 2″ in front of the prolongation of the line of the lips, and the back stay should lie in the chin groove under the snaffle. And however the back stay is designed, see that the buckle is at the side of the mouth when fitted so that it does not press into the bone at the back of the jaw when tight. A buckle pressing into the bone of the chin groove can really torment a horse.

The headstall supporting the drop noseband should be at least $\frac{5}{8}$″ wide. If less, it will bend and permit the front stay to drop or droop too low.

Horses do not like a drop noseband, particularly at first, and you may find it profitable to remove it whenever you rest the animal. In any case, the horse will appreciate its removal.

As drop nosebands are fidgety things to re-buckle, I personally do not thread the headstall through the browband but lay it over the top of the bridle. Then, when the horse is given a rest-break at any time, it can be slipped off over the ears without unbuckling—provided that when both removing and replacing the band, the back stay is in the chin groove when the front stay is slipped over the muzzle.

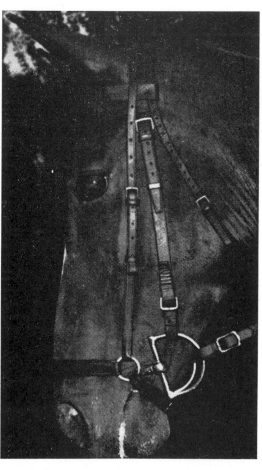

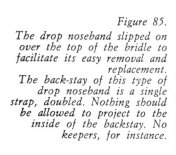

Figure 85.
The drop noseband slipped on over the top of the bridle to facilitate its easy removal and replacement.
The back-stay of this type of drop noseband is a single strap, doubled. Nothing should be allowed to project to the inside of the backstay. No keepers, for instance.

DO NOT fit the drop noseband ABOVE the snaffle at any time, as serious pinching of the lips occurs when the rein is tightened. CHECK, by running your finger from side to side under the strap, to see that no hair has been trapped in the buckle when adjusting the noseband.

It is seldom, if ever, that the use of a drop noseband is justified when used with any type of curb bit. There is not sufficient room in the chin groove for both curb chain and noseband.

Nothing New in Drop Noseband

Major F. Dwyer in his book of some 100 years ago, spoke of the drop noseband which he called the "Reithalfter" and concluded:

> "It must, however, be well understood that this halter is not intended to be permanently employed; its great value is that it enables us, by preventing the young horse from escaping the action of a mild snaffle mouthpiece, to avoid the necessity of employing sharper ones during the period of training or handling. When this is once over, we may lay aside our halter (drop noseband) and use either a plain snaffle or a curb bit. A plain smooth-mouthed snaffle aided by the drop noseband will be found to answer every purpose and afford the best possible means of mouthing young animals."

The above quotation is well worth study.

Figure 86. Mr. R. H. Hayes with his "Hannibal," a good performer in Three-Day-Events, with a quite effective drop noseband.

We show it here to illustrate the fact that the further forward the supporting strap, the easier it is to keep the front-stay well above the nostrils while allowing the back-stay to pass below the snaffle without displacing it.

However it is NOT recommended that the headstall be looped around the noseband as in this instance. Nothing should project to the inside of a noseband. It is much to be preferred if the headstall be stitched to the OUTSIDE of the noseband and the stitches on the inside be "boned" smooth.

If one was to adopt the sloped noseband shown, why not stitch the noseband to the headstall at the appropriate position and at the requisite angle. The buckle to be just behind the line of the lips and on the near side.

Cross-over Drop Noseband

There is a type of drop noseband which comes from the back of the jaw to the face, crosses, and passes around the chin groove. This seems to be quite good for horses after they have finished teething. The upper part passes right over the molars, so could worry any horse with tooth trouble (see Figure 83 page 111).

In one type of drop noseband in use recently in this country, the back-stay consists of a single strap, such as shown in Fig. 85. This is quite satisfactory, provided it has no keepers to project inward and worry the lower jaw.

Whatever may be said against a drop noseband it has this very great advantage over an ordinary nose band—IT STAYS WELL CLEAR OF THOSE SHARP MOLAR TEETH.

CHAPTER 17

TONGUE OVER THE BIT

Precautions to Prevent the Development of this Habit

Simple precautions: Correcting the tongue-over-the-bit habit:
U.S. Cavalry recommendations: A stockman's recommendations:
British Army recommendations: Prevention better than cure!

Although I recommend the ordinary jointed snaffle, most types have a troublesome fault in that the centre of the bit drops and hangs much lower inside the mouth than at the sides. Unless it is drawn quite high into the mouth, the centre joint hangs too low and the young horse, who finds a bit strange in any case, plays with it with his tongue and not infrequently develops the habit of getting his tongue over the bit.

The tongue-over-the-bit habit is not only annoying and unsightly, but is one that can lead to much trouble. The horse tosses and fidgets with the bit incessantly and once the habit is established, in a bad case the horse then starts lolling his tongue out of his mouth in a most unsightly manner.

Some say it is impossible to rid the horse of the habit; certainly it is not easy. Experienced riders are always alert to take every precaution to prevent the formation of this most vexatious trick.

Prevent Your Horse Acquiring the Vice

The horse's tongue habits are formed during the first few weeks he is bitted; and once formed, good or bad, they will not easily be broken. So it is important that during these first few weeks we do not use a bit that drops in the centre, as do so many types of the jointed snaffle or, if we are compelled to use such a bit, we should fit it quite high in the horse's mouth. This latter alternative of course has obvious disadvantages—for the horse.

There are several types of jointed snaffles on the market that do not drop at the centre joint, and one of these should be used for the first few weeks of the breaking period. If such a snaffle is not available, a jointed pelham will do very well if the mouthpiece is reasonably thick. The mouthpiece of a jointed pelham does not drop in the centre and if the curb chain and hooks are removed (they can easily be replaced), it acts in exactly the same manner as a snaffle—indeed, it becomes a snaffle (see Figure 63 page 91 and Figure 15 page 27).

Simple Precautions

The tongue over the bit habit is a very real fault that among other things will slow the horse's training progress considerably. It is well worth any precaution we can take to prevent the formation of the habit.

It is not unusual for any youngster to get his tongue over the bit in the early days after breaking. It is usually easy to tell it has happened, for the horse immediately starts tossing and fussing with his head—he is then trying to get his tongue back UNDER the bit. He tosses his head and if he can't get it back, twists his head so that one side of his mouth is higher than the other for a moment or two, and opens his mouth wide. He is most uncomfortable when he feels the bit under his tongue.

But, if you dismount and put him right or he gets it right himself, he will almost immediately try to get his tongue OVER the bit again.

If you don't take immediate steps to prevent it, he will eventually spend most of his time, from then on, trying to get his tongue the other side of the bit—whichever that might be.

Take alarm immediately you find him starting to get his tongue over the bit. Put his tongue back under and raise the bit, even to the point of making him uncomfortable should he succeed in getting it over again. In fact it is wise always to have the snaffle fitted very well up in the mouth of a young horse—at least until his tongue habits are formed. This period covers a month or two if he is ridden fairly regularly. Once he has grown accustomed to keeping the bit in its proper place he seldom alters, no matter what you put in his mouth or how high or how low it is.

A drop noseband is recommended if it seems the habit is forming. For the young horse it has these two virtues at least—one, it tends to prevent the tongue over the bit habit forming; and two, it does not interfere with growing teeth—as do ordinary nosebands. More has been said in Chapters 2, 4 and 14 on nosebands, about this pressure near or on the gums when a young horse is teething.

Correcting the Tongue-over-the-bit Habit

It is a very difficult practice to cure. You can buy bits designed to prevent the horse doing it; they usually consist of an additional attachment to the centre of the mouthpiece that is then buckled or tied over the nose or on to the noseband. This fills the space above the mouthpiece when the horse opens his mouth to get the tongue over, and so makes it difficult for him to do so. You might try one of these if a high snaffle and a drop noseband prove a failure, but I am told they are seldom successful.

Almost everything I am writing I have tried and proved, but I have had little experience with this vice—for vice it is—so I will re-print here the

RECOMMENDATIONS (if they amount to recommendations) *of the U.S. CAVALRY.* Here they are:

"About the only solution is to tie the tongue in the mouth, making it impossible to pull it back from the proper position under the bit. A piece of cloth tape about ¾" wide can be used for the purpose.

Cut a transversal slit part way across the tape and slip one end through the slit, thus forming a noose. The noose is put around the horse's tongue and drawn as tightly as possible without cutting off blood circulation. The two ends are then run down and tied underneath the lower jaw with enough tension to keep the tongue in its proper place.

Another method which is sometimes effective and which does not involve the actual tying of the tongue, is as follows:

"Tie a piece of tape to the snaffle bit at the joint of the mouthpiece, having the two ends of the tape of equal length, before putting the bridle on the horse. The two loose ends come out of the corners of the mouth and are tied to the two cheek pieces of the bridle, or to the noseband at the middle of the horse's face. It works more easily if a small hole is punched in the noseband, running one end of the tape through the noseband and tying it to the other."

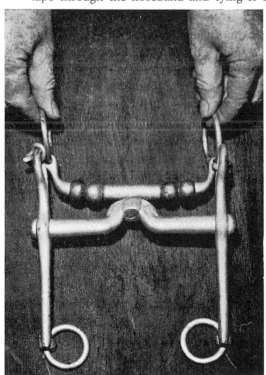

Figure 87.
"Mowhawk Patent" is stamped on this Bit or Pelham (one of several in my collection that I have never used.) It is of good proportions and complies with all the rules of good bitting. I would like to have the designer's views on it. It is really the two bits of a double bridle joined together at the centre in a manner that would appear to make it difficult, if not impossible, for the horse to get his tongue over it. It would need to be fitted in exactly the same manner as the Bit and bridoon of a double bridle.
The bridoon-like section is shaped like the Scamperdale (Figure 67 page 93). Much narrower than the Bit mouthpiece but with its ends well thrown out. A well made bit. I almost wish I had a horse with a tongue-over-the-bit habit to try it on.

121

This last device stops the centre of the mouthpiece from dropping in the mouth. For the same reason, I recommend the non-drop type of mouthpiece in the early tongue habit-forming period of training. The horse hates having his tongue over the bit but once he has the habit it's like smoking or biting your nails — you do it although you don't want to — even though you hate it.

Use the jointed snaffle, but select a type that does not drop in the centre as it has an advantage during these early months and no disadvantages later.

AN AUSTRALIAN STOCKMAN'S RECOMMENDATION

Here is another method which has been strongly recommended to me as a "sure cure."

> "Put an old bridle on the horse with a smooth jointed ring snaffle in the mouth, and leave it on for several days. Don't take it off for feeding or for any other reason; the best thing of all is to turn him out to grass with it on. He has to keep his tongue in the right place to eat and it seems he accepts that as its normal position after a while."

This is so little trouble that it is well worth giving it a go.

N.B. THE BRITISH ARMY RECOMMENDATION READS:

> "The snaffle should be put on for an hour a day in the stable and the horse should be allowed to feed with it on. This will be found specially useful in preventing the development of a tendency to get the tongue over the bit."

If ever there is a matter in which *"prevention is better than cure,"* the tongue-over-the-bit habit is it. Act quickly at the first sign of its development.

CHAPTER 18

OBTAINING A FAST HALT

How horse stops to maximum advantage: Horse Must have warning:
Big difference between "tug" and "pull": Horse can detect difference
in fine pressures: Pain will not stop a horse

In many respects the control of a horse can be compared to the driving of
a car — but not in stopping. *You* can't stop a horse from his back, you
can only do something that may induce or coerce HIM to stop himself.

The skill of a rider is shown in his ability to obtain co-operation from
his horse and in his ability to induce his mount to put all his efforts into
stopping himself.

A good quiet and sudden stop requires great muscular effort on the part
of the horse and considerable strength, particularly in the loins. Not all
horses have this strength and without it they are incapable of the effort.
Not only must the horse have the strength but he requires and must have
to give of his best, a moment's warning of the rider's requirements so that
he can adjust his balance for the effort needed.

Re-adjustment of the horse's balance is an essential preliminary to any
quick decrease of pace. It must PRECEDE the check in pace.

Fast Stop Should be Obtained from Hindquarters

A horse that is hurt by the bit tends to fight for his head, poke his nose
out and "prop" to a halt using his front legs to decrease the pace, with a
subsequent lowering of the forehand. He just cannot stop quickly in this
manner, for among other things he just does not have the required strength
in the forelimbs. On the other hand this great stress on his forelegs tends
to make him "break down."

When the horse uses his hindlegs to stop or check his pace, he tucks his
hindlegs under him and this lowers the quarters and "sits him down." This
is the way first class polo ponies and stock horses stop; they tend to sit
down and more or less slide. On any polo ground you will find skid marks
yards long, where the hind feet have torn up the turf.

123

One advantage of stopping in this manner is that the hind legs, having been brought under the body to stop, are then in a position for instant starting or turning.

Remember: the rider does not have to teach the horse how to stop; the horse knows how. The rider's concern should be to use the reins in a manner that will not distract the horse or provoke him into fighting the bit.

Must Have Warning

If the horse gets a warning a fraction of a second before the demand is made — before he feels the bit — it gives him the chance he must have to prepare for the halt required and to adjust his balance for the effort demanded. This is where the loose weighted rein on a curb bit becomes effective, the horse can detect the movement that precedes the pressure of the mouthpiece — I refer here to reins having a short length of chain at the Bit, spoken of in Chapter 13 when discussing "Cowboy" Bits.

The rein should be shortened, not pulled. The difference is: a "pull" is a *continuing movement* of the hand to the rear. A "shortening" is a small and *limited* movement of the hand to the rear, after which the hand remains still, resistant, or may yield again immediately. If the increased tension proves to be insufficient, a second shortening is made after a fractional pause. In the case of a trained but disobedient horse, the rider might then become a little sharp, but with a young horse which still has to learn, the signal is only repeated — without increasing its strength. The feel of the reins should be a signal, not an application of force.

Of course, we become sharper with the reins if, when we have done the right thing, the horse, knowing what we want, takes things too easily. But even in this instance, extra force should not be used. In such a case, the reins are used with short sharp and very limited tugs — the bit gives the bars of the mouth LIGHT TAPS rather than long hard pulls. The sharpness should be of a disciplinary nature rather than a test of strength.

Big Difference Between "Tug" and "Pull"

A tug is a momentary pull, one of short duration. We terminate the pull, thus making it into a tug. It is repeated rather than continued. Continuing it converts a tug into a pull. If we were preparing a school table for horsemen we might include: "several tugs (joined together) make one pull." A tug is a LIGHT shortening of the rein which is terminated immediately but may be repeated if necessary.

The message you have to get through to the horse's brain is: "Go a little slower, yield ever so little, and the pressure of the bit will decrease."

Many riders fail to grasp the fact that the horse has to be *taught* this. It is worse than useless to increase the pressure and punish the animal if he fails to understand. It will only confuse and perhaps panic him.

There ARE increases and decreases of pressure, but they are most minute. Never lose sight of the fact that at your end of the reins you have soft pliable leather on a finger padded with flesh; at his end he has steel resting on a ridge of bone as thin as the back of a knife, and covered only with a layer of most sensitive skin (Figures 54 and 55 page 79). To get some idea of his situation you need to place a bit on the bone of your own nose, get someone to drive you forward and then guide and control you with the reins.

Horse Can Detect Difference in Fine Pressures

If you try putting yourself in his position, you may realise what I mean when I compare the horse's mouth with the keyboard of a piano. Each different half-note is readily detectable from the ones above and below it. You don't need to jump up the keyboard in leaps of ten notes at a time to detect a difference; nor does your horse. He can detect (steel on bone at his end, don't forget) smaller differences than you, with accuracy, can make.

PAIN WILL NOT STOP A HORSE — you have proved that yourself probably, and although pain as a disciplinary measure is sometimes useful, it is only so when skilfully applied as part of a considered plan. It is the horse's brain you have to influence; from his brain he, and only he, controls his limbs and efforts.

The great rider is the one who can convey his wishes to his mount without in any way interfering with the animal's freedom as he attempts to carry out those wishes.

If you use your hands suddenly and roughly, the horse is given no chance to avoid the pain — even if he knows what you want and is keen to do it. The first thing he knows is a sudden sharp pain: how can he avoid what he has already experienced? He must have some warning.

Would — could — an athlete at the start of a race start quicker if you suddenly stuck a pin into his rump instead of calling "Ready? Go"?

CHAPTER 19

ON ONE-SIDED MOUTHED OR "LUGGING" HORSES

Matter of horsemanship rather than special bit

I have deliberately omitted dealing with this most baffling defect in a mouth — the horse with "a hard mouth one side." It is almost impossible to turn some horses with this trouble in one direction while they answer most readily to the other.

Some carry their heads off to one side the whole time, some only when the reins are tightened — and you can't pull them straight.

The harder you pull on the "hard" side of the animal's mouth the harder he will pull against you. The left side is most commonly "hard," so that the majority of horses carry their heads to the right of straight, and, as I have said throughout — "the harder you pull, the harder he pulls."

The correction of a one-sided mouthed horse in my experience, is more a matter of horsemanship — equitation — than of a special bit, and it is out of the range of this work, therefore, for the subject to be dealt with fully.

You can buy special bits for "luggers," as they are called, and some even have spikes of varying lengths inside the cheek-bar of the bit. They sometimes lead to the animal bolting, and in any case are effective only for a very short time — if at all. I do not recommend them, and strongly advise against their use.

I have said the matter is too involved to deal with fully here. But I will say something, and perhaps it will start you thinking on the right lines.

Treat the one-sided mouth, not as if one side was as "hard as iron," but as if the OTHER side was exceptionally "soft," and very sensitive. Isn't that much more likely to be the case? Isn't it more likely that he is trying to free the sensitive side of his mouth from rein pressure, rather than trying to get more pressure on the less sensitive side?

I would say too that "hanging on" to the *hard* side is about the worst thing you can do in such a case, and if you are not convinced that horses resist pain and force, you will be if ever you ride or drive a bad "lugger"!

Short, light, and slight tugs with the rein on the hard side of the mouth will be found more effective than a long sustained pull (see what is said in Chapter 18 re "tugs"). But the real answer to the problem lies in the use of the *other rein,* the one on the "soft" side. This should NOT be loosened, but HELD. The horse must not be permitted to profit — escape the bit pressure on that side — by taking his head that way when he is not asked to do it.

You might say, "But you have said 'discourage that which you do not want' so if he takes his head to one side, say the right, the other rein, the left, discourages him."

Yes, I do say that, and I also say: "Encourage that which you want." If you loosen the rein on the soft side at the same time as you tighten the rein on the hard side, aren't you doing the two opposites at the same time — discouraging the fault with the one rein and encouraging the same defect with the other rein?

Think it over; think it over.

I hope to write "A theory of horse control" sometime — when I can get around to it. I say "a theory" not "the theory." There are lots of ways to produce an effect — a fact I am continually having to notice. Keep an open mind, and when that book does get written, prepare for some shocks! Not, of course, that there is anything new for me to write; the facts are all well known, but remember a school of thought, a country, a company, only has an advantage over its rivals so long as its valuable knowledge and know-how remains secret. Not everyone tries to pass on to others ALL they know.

Figure 88. The "Half-moon Lugging Snaffle." The term "Lugging" is in common use in trotting circles in Australia and refers to horses that are one-sided mouthed. They take hold of the bit on one side of the mouth, set their heads the other and really hang on.
A very difficult mouth to deal with and too big a subject to be more than touched on in this work. The half-bars should be pointed downward as shown.
Do NOT use any bit or other appliance with spikes or points. They are cruel, ineffective, and drive the horse to desperation.

CHAPTER 20

FINAL ADVICE

"Confucius, he says . . . ."

I hope what I have written will help you in your dealings with horses. This work is meant to be a reference book, one you should keep. You are almost sure to need to refer to it again and again.

I have stressed the avoidance of painful bits of all kinds, but I certainly do not say: "Never hurt a horse." The touch of a spur, the flick of a whip, a short jolt with the bit — these things have their place in training and are valuable when used with discretion and moderation.

If you are just, moderate and deliberate, the horse will be none the worse for it. The real value of punishment comes from the quiet friendliness that should follow THE MOMENT THE HORSE TENDS TO BEHAVE BETTER. Notice I always say "better"—not "perfectly." Improvement leads to perfection if it continues.

AIM AT PERFECTION: BUT FROM DAY TO DAY ASK
ONLY FOR IMPROVEMENT OR SOME LITTLE PROGRESS.

Encourage the horse whenever he makes the slightest progress. Be tolerant with his mistakes, discourage him in them; but don't punish him unless you are sure he knows it is wrong. Then be INSTANT and APPROPRIATE. Better, far better, not to punish him at all if you do it even seconds later. He will not associate the punishment with his misdeed if the punishment comes too late. Remember, if you sit on a tack you don't need someone to tell you to jump up, you know instantly that you have done wrong. The result follows so closely on the action that you cannot fail to associate them. So it is with our horse; the closer our re-action is to his action, the easier it is for his mind to associate them.

Learn to feel, practice "FEEL." Feel for his mouth, practice feeling for the movement of his legs and the changes of balance that *always precede* the movements of the legs. Keep in mind that he cannot move a leg until he takes weight off it. Practice feeling for the changes of balance that PRE-CEDE movement and which can be discouraged or encouraged, at that stage, with a change of pressure by leg or bit equal to a fraction of a note on the piano keyboard.

So often people say when they see a difficult horse being handled with ease: "But WHAT DO YOU *DO?* I can't see you doing anything!"

It is the tiny, minute changes of pressure at the exact moment, that are so effective. When feeling for his mouth, while being conscious of how much more sensitive his mouth is than your fingers, you must, nevertheless, concentrate on what you feel AT YOUR FINGERS. FEEL at your end what is happening at his, and you do this at the finger where the rein first touches your hand on its way from the horse's mouth.

Don't *think* of his end of the reins — *feel* your end. *Feel.* Concentrate on "feel."

If you were Stronger, Could you Do Better?

If you think so still, then my efforts in this work have failed. If you think that force, strength or pain, will stop a horse, how do you explain that no-one has thought to provide a machine or device such as a windlass or block and tackle fixed to the saddle, capable of applying all the force and power that you yourself lack?

I have spent many years with difficult and problem horses — horses spoiled by others. Some have been quite easily put right, but often the horse has not been worth (in cash) the risk and time spent on it — so often it is the case of: "He's mine; I couldn't have him 'put down' — and I couldn't sell him!" One gets no prizes for doing such work — only a good deal of personal satisfaction.

Each horse adds to experience and know-how, and it is in the light of this experience that I have tried to explain the "whys" and "hows" and principles of good bitting.

Of course I have not said all there is to be said, but what I have said has been proved with a wide personal experience — a very wide experience. To those who cannot agree with all I have said, well, I'm still learning!

In conclusion may I quote an old teacher who lived a long time ago, Confucius, who is said to have said:

> "If I have a pupil and I tell him 25% and he doesn't go away and work out the other 75%, I don't trouble any more with him."

So battle on, Friend; the other 75% is all yours.

INDEX